# OF DOGS AND MEN

## FIFTY YEARS IN THE ANTARCTIC

**The Illustrated Story of
the Dogs of the British
Antarctic Survey
1944 - 1994**

# OF DOGS AND MEN

## FIFTY YEARS IN THE ANTARCTIC

The Illustrated Story of
the Dogs of the British
Antarctic Survey
1944 - 1994

## KEVIN WALTON AND RICK ATKINSON

Foreword by HRH The Prince of Wales

First published in Great Britain 1996 by
Images Publishing (Malvern) Ltd,
The Wells House, Holywell Road, Malvern Wells,
Worcestershire WR14 4LH

British Library Cataloguing in Publication Data

A catalogue record for this book is available
from the British Library

ISBN 1 897817 55 X

Every copy of this book when sold brings 20% of the royalty to
the Fuchs Foundation, a fund set up as a tribute to Sir Vivian Fuchs
to help disadvantaged young people find adventure for themselves.
This royalty is administered through the British Antarctic Survey.

Designed by Anita Sherwood
Produced by Images Publishing (Malvern) Ltd.
Printed and Bound in Great Britain by BPC Ltd, Bristol.

# CONTENTS

This book was conceived as a tribute to the late Ted Bingham whose skill and enthusiasm for dog driving became a tradition and feature of the British Antarctic Survey for 50 years. We dedicate it to the dogs – our transport, our life savers and our all-round companions. They were terrific.

Day after day, week after week, they had moved further into a great white world that only the wind and the snow gods knew – nine dogs pulling a sledge with a driver skiing alongside, followed at a distance of a few hundred yards by another team of dogs and driver. They were twenty living, breathing units passing through an otherwise sterile wilderness, changing it not at all, save for their tracks that would soon disappear.

'Aaahh, boys,' the first man called. The words were sufficient. There was no need to apply the foot brake, for the dogs were as tired as their drivers, and only too ready to stop. At once they dropped down in the snow and curled themselves up, heads resting on paws facing downwind, tails wrapped around, with tips covering noses. There was none of the growling and readiness to fight of a fresh team, these dogs were exhausted; but still within each was the willingness to pull a load – that spark of adventure that makes the husky so different from other dogs.

'They've had it – poor devils,' said the driver of the first team. The second man nodded as he crouched on the lee side of the sledge. 'Eighteen miles south of base,' he muttered. The two men did not talk much; they had been on the trail too long to waste energy on unnecessary conversation. Each one sat hunched in his windproofs, chewing a last piece of chocolate. Too tired to relax and think of other places and other days when all is going well and bodies and minds are fresh, they had only one thought – those eighteen bloody miles that still lay ahead and the blizzard that was threatening, with no food left to sit it out.

After a few moments both men stood up, as if both had known that this was the exact minute at which they had to start out again. After sledging and camping with the same person for many weeks, thoughts seemed to pass backward and forward without words being spoken. Each driver gripped the handlebars of his sledge. 'Now dogs.' The teams stirred, heads looking up and around. 'Now dogs, huit!' With a twisting heave on the sledge from its driver, each team once again slid off northwards. Behind them the steady hiss of the drifting snow and the moan of the wind were the only sounds. Soon the tracks of dogs and men were filled with snow and again nothing lived in this land. And yet because for a few brief moments life had breathed here, the wilderness would never be as lonely again.

*Ken Pauson, Admiralty Bay, 1947/49*

[Overleaf]
(Photo: Ben Osborne,
Rothera, 1989/92)

ST. JAMES'S PALACE

The departure of the last remaining huskies from Antarctica marks
the end of an era, and is perhaps a sad, but appropriate, moment
for the publication of this fascinating book.  It will always be
difficult for those who have not shared the experience to
understand the pure delight of driving behind dogs and being
utterly dependent on them for life itself, but there can be no
doubt that the huskies made a great difference to the morale and
well-being of those who lived and worked with them.

It is sad and extraordinary that environmental arguments are
being advanced in support of the decision to remove the huskies.
For many people, life in Antarctica without dogs will somehow
seem incomplete; there is no doubt that the combination of men
and dogs working together in Antarctica is a unique part of our
heritage.  It would be hard to imagine a more sustainable or less
environmentally-damaging means of transport and I hope that a
wiser generation may allow their return at some time in the
future.  If they do, this book will be an invaluable guide to a
vanished way of life.

# INTRODUCTION

This is a story of dogs and men and of the partnership that can exist between them. Huskies were far more than just haulage animals that gave us the ability to travel and work in some of the most demanding, and beautiful, places on earth. They were our companions, whose individual likes and dislikes we soon learned and respected, who willingly gave us their loyalty and lent us their strength, and who cheerfully shared both good days and bad. Undoubtedly present day adventurers will still enjoy their time in Antarctica; but to share that wilderness with a petrol-driven snow machine will always be a poor substitute for the husky. To sit alone in a remote and beautiful location allows one to experience a special kind of spiritual awareness. Add one stoic husky, gaze into its eyes and see the reflection of the mountains beyond, and you have the ingredients to considerably intensify the experience. This book is therefore an attempt to record a way of life that has disappeared. We hope that it explains why so many of us developed an affection and respect for dogs that is far deeper than the most sentimental would have believed possible.

There are many people who have contributed to the book. When the idea of writing it was put forward we were overwhelmed with offers of help by way of pictures, stories and diary extracts. Sadly only a fraction of these have found space in the book. Our thanks go to those whose contributions have not been included, as much as to those who have. Thanks must also go to the Royal Geographical Society and to the descendants of Otto Nordenskjöld, who, at short notice, allowed pictures from their collections to be included in Chapter Two.

There are three people who deserve special thanks. Firstly, 'Anne' Todd, secretary to the Survey for its first 35 years, whose encyclopaedic knowledge of people, places and names was so valuable in the early stages. She has also put together the facts and figures that form the appendices of the book. Catherine Whiting took on the almost impossible job as publishing editor for a book that was no more than an idea in the back of our minds. People who have worked with BAS, collectively referred to as 'Fids', are better known for their drive and enthusiasm than for their literary skills. If the book has style and coherence she must take much of the credit; if it has not, we must take the blame for not listening to her. Last, but by no means least, is Clifford 'Doggie' Hubbard, the well known author, collector and seller of dog books, whose *Working Dogs of the World* and *Dogs in Britain* are regarded as classics. We visited him at his home in Aberystwyth where, against the background of his library of some 20,000 dog books, he gave us enthusiastic encouragement. It was he who emphasised that this should not be a book of instruction on driving huskies, rather the simple story of what *we* did and why. We hope that is what we have achieved.

*Kevin Walton and Rick Atkinson, January 1996*

# CHAPTER ONE
# THE HUSKY

*'The character of the husky exemplified the characteristics that some of us aspired to attain — extreme patience and endurance in miserable conditions, and a love of hard work for no reward but its own sake 'til he dropped in his tracks.'*

Peter Gibbs, Stonington, 1956/58

The partnership between man and dog goes back far into history. Evidence found in Arctic Canada and Greenland suggests that Eskimo huskies have been pulling sledges for the Inuit people of Chukotka as long ago as 50 BC. These were working animals, wild and wolf-like; but they were highly valued and essential for survival.

In comparatively recent times kennel clubs around the world have classified husky breeds: the Alaskan Malamute, a large, powerful freight dog originating from the Alaskan Malamute Eskimos; the smaller, often faster, blue-eyed Siberian, from the Chukchi people of northern Siberia; the Samoyed, a small dog with white fur, originating from the Samoyed people of eastern Siberia; and last, but not least, the Eskimo husky from Arctic Canada and Greenland.

The severe climate and limited interaction with the outside world has led to the Eskimo husky evolving as a distinct breed, a good deal more hardy than others, with a stocky build, a dense inner fur and a coarse outer thatch that allow it to survive in the most hostile of environments. A descendant of the wolf, the Eskimo husky maintains a wolf-like appearance, but is larger boned, with a broader head, a shorter snout, and a tightly curled tail. Legend has it that in order for the breed to remain true, a bitch on heat would be tied to a tree where the wolf would pay her a visit. A shortage of trees – and indeed wolves – in Antarctica was to render this tradition impractical; yet many of the wolf's instincts were carried down through generations of what we now think of as 'Antarctic huskies'.

During the early exploration of Canada and Alaska, European explorers and settlers relied heavily upon dog teams for their winter transportation. Any available dogs would do, as long as they could pull; in consequence, numerous breeds not normally associated with sledge-pulling were introduced, loosely referred to as 'Alaskan huskies'. Although of predominantly Eskimo husky origin, the dogs of the British Antarctic Survey were a mixed breed, and almost certainly related to these mongrels.

Mongrel or pedigree, the 'perfect husky' is an elusive concept. Dogs, like people, have their good days and their bad days. Some work well for one driver and not at all for another. Some work well when placed beside a particular dog or at a particular point in the gang line. Some work well when the going is tough, others when the pace is fast and even. Certainly the dogs of the British Antarctic Survey were not perfect. Amongst a typical team there would be old timers, slow, becoming arthritic, but reliable and steady; young pups, learning the ropes, easily distracted and tiring quickly; there would be leaders and followers; heroes and cowards. As well as this, they came in all shapes and sizes; some of them were dreadful fighters and there were as many different gaits as there were dogs. Like most things in life it was a compromise. What mattered to a driver with so many miles of difficult terrain to cover was the spirit and the will to work – qualities for which huskies are renowned. As teams, they were capable of achieving remarkable feats of endurance – up to 30 miles a day, hauling two or three times their own body weight, and demanding only a little food and affection in return.

*(Photo: Michael Skidmore, Halley, 1967/69)*

'Huskies possess a unique drive both to travel and to pull. They are large and demanding animals and for this reason make difficult pets; but as working dogs they are ideal. Their notorious flaw is a tendency to fight whenever the opportunity arises – not because they are naturally vicious but because, like their ancestor the wolf, they have a need to exert their authority or maintain their position in the pack.'

*Peter Forster, Stonington, 1957/61*

Brothers 'Spike' and 'Norman' at eight months old.

*(Photo: Simon Fraser, Rothera, 1981/1984)*

'Actually it is more comfortable than it looks! "Eccles", like all the dogs, would curl up with his back to the wind and let the drifting snow build up around him. The snow actually provided an insulation layer and the dogs would only break out of their little nests for very good reasons – such as feeding time.'

*Roger Scott, Stonington, 1972/75*

'For me, each new experience exults still higher our friends the huskies. Nine mounds of snow were the only sign of their existence this morning. On my approach, each mound cracked to disclose a black nose and an icy face. Then, like nine grenades, the mounds exploded and nine well-salivated tongues competed for the doubtful honour of licking my gloved hand. Yes, it was well worth emerging from the warmth of the sleeping bag, if only for those canine affections.'

*Peter Forster, Stonington, 1957/61*

'"Singing" was obviously a very necessary part of the dogs' social order, and tended to occur just before they settled down for the night. One dog would begin a low "wooing" sound, followed by another and then another, each with a slightly different pitch. The bitches would come in with a higher, lilting and often longer "woo-oo". After a minute or so, when every dog was singing his or her part, there was a great crescendo followed by an abrupt silence as though they were observing a conductor's command to stop. Who signalled that stop? I wondered. I would love to know.'

*Nick Cox, Rothera, 1979/81*

*(Photo: Ian Sykes, Stonington, 1967/69)*

'Although the dogs could be savage in their behaviour to each other, with only a few exceptions they crave affection and attention from their drivers. If caught unawares, a hundredweight of dog could easily knock a man over, but their only intent was to give you a thorough licking.'

*Rob Collister, Stonington, 1971/73*

*(Photo: Neil Orr, Hope Bay, 1958/61)*

*(Photo: Ian McMorrin, Stonington, 1962/64)*

Ken Blaiklock at Stonington.
It was important not to show favouritism to one particular dog. They all
liked to be thanked and receive a bit of fuss after a hard day's slog.

*(Photo, Peter Clarkson, Halley, 1968/75)*

Peter Clarkson and 'Boo-Boo'.

'The huskies moulted in summertime, and this was very noticeable with "Boo-Boo", whose coat
changed from magnificent orange to a deep brown colour. I was more interested in his attitude,
though. All the other dogs would rush towards me, barking and rearing up their hind legs to put their
paws on my shoulders. Boo-Boo was very reserved and for several weeks as I walked towards him, he
would retreat to the opposite side of his circle on the span. He was seven years old and we wondered
if perhaps he had been ill-treated in the past. Anyway, I began walking to the end of his chain so that
he could not escape. Gradually he came to accept my presence until eventually he would come
towards me when he saw me. Whatever had been his fear, I had managed to overcome it with
patience and we never looked back.'

'Morag' dressed for action.

*(Photo: Rod Pashley, Adelaide, 1969/70)*

'Wensen' of the Hairybreeks team.

*(Photo: Michael Skidmore, Halley, 1967/69)*

'Though the dogs had wolf blood in their ancestry, they were
very happy around humans and we around them. There was
only one time – a cold moonlit night camping on the Stancomb
Wills Glacier – when they frightened me. That night I awoke very
suddenly at about 2 a.m. It was dead quiet: no wind, no shuffling
of dogs, nor rattling of chains, no reason in fact why I should
have woken up. I listened for a while, but still heard nothing.
I looked across at my tent partner Tony; he was fast asleep. For
some unexplained reason I felt incredibly uneasy, and, very
quietly, so as not to disturb him, I sat up in my sleeping bag
and opened the tent door. Despite there having been no noise,
every one of the dogs was sitting upright, their bright eyes staring
at me. And even when they saw me they remained completely
motionless. A cold fear gripped me, and I sat back rapidly in
the tent. It was the strangest feeling I have ever experienced.'

*Dave Fletcher, Halley, 1978*

*(Photo: Roger Scott, Stonington, 1972/75)*

# CHAPTER TWO
# DOGS IN ANTARCTICA

*'Look kindly on these Thy creatures for we are entirely dependent on them and they with us are utterly dependent on Thee.'*

The Reverend Launcelot Fleming's 'Prayer for the dogs',
British Graham Land Expedition, 1936

For centuries Antarctica was just a part of seafarers' folklore – the 'end of the world' that they had never seen but were sure that existed. Only the hardiest of sailors would brave the wild, stormy waters of the southern ocean, and beyond that, frozen sea and heavy pack ice formed a seemingly impenetrable barrier to the place they dreamed about. It was not until 1820 that the Russian explorer Thaddeus von Bellingshausen recorded a sighting of land; and the following year Captain John Davis, drawn on by the search for whales and seals, recorded a landing on the Continent itself. Where he landed is uncertain, for he and his men worked in secrecy, afraid that others might spoil their new hunting ground.

Seventy-four years later the Norwegian-born Australian Carsten Borchgrevink landed near Cape Adare with the idea of making the first exploratory trips of the area. In 1899 he returned with 75 huskies and 11 men, built a small base hut on the shore and prepared to sit out the winter before embarking on travel inland. In the event, dogs and men did very little beyond surviving, but they proved that it could be done.

In 1902 Dr Otto Nordenskjöld made remarkably good use of sledge dogs during the first exploration of the east coast of the Antarctic Peninsula. The 380-mile return journey from Snow Hill Island to Borchgrevink Nunatak was made in 33 days – remarkable even by today's standards. That same year came Captain Scott and the first of the big national expeditions. Scott brought a few dogs with him, but no one who knew how to drive them; consequently, the dogs contributed very little to his expedition. He was followed, in 1907,

by Ernest Shackleton who brought Manchurian Ponies and nine dogs. The ponies proved disastrously ineffective; their food was bulky and difficult to transport; they were heavier than dogs, more prone to breaking through crevasses and practically impossible to extract once this had happened.

In 1911 the competent and very experienced Roald Amundsen sailed south in the *Fram*, and nine men and over 100 dogs were landed on the shelf ice in the Bay of Whales. The story of his subsequent journey to the South Pole is now well known. He left base with 55 dogs, intentionally killed 41 at various stages during the journey, feeding them to those that remained, and returned to his base with 14 dogs as sleek and as fit as the day they had left. He covered 1,860 miles in 89 days – an extraordinary demonstration of how effectively huskies could work in Antarctica.

Shortly after the *Fram* had reached the Continent, the *Terra Nova* landed Captain Scott at his old base in McMurdo Sound, along with a large party of men, 23 Siberian huskies and 10 Manchurian ponies. In addition to extensive scientific work, Scott also planned to make a bid for the Pole, and this time was wise enough to include in his party a trained dog driver, the Norwegian Trygve Gran. In spite of this precaution, from the point of view of efficient travel the expedition was a disaster. Five men hauled the sledge to the Pole, only to find that Amundsen had beaten them to it.

A year later the Australian Sir Douglas Mawson, who had served with Shackleton in 1907, went south on his own expedition. He took 21 huskies bred from

In 1902 Dr Otto Nordenskjöld, Lieutenant J M Sobral and a seaman named Ole Jonassen made a remarkable 380-mile journey using dogs. This was the first properly recorded journey made in Antarctica, and for many years the longest.

Amundsen's dogs, together with 15 men, of whom two were experienced drivers. The dogs worked very well but the expedition met with disaster when one of the men, seven dogs and a loaded sledge fell into a crevasse. All were lost. Desperately low on rations, the men were forced to eat the remaining dogs, one by one, in an attempt to survive the return journey. Sadly only Mawson himself made it back to base.

In 1914 Shackleton returned to the Antarctic with an ambitious plan to cross the Continent from the south end of the Weddell Sea to the Bay of Whales, and for the first time to use dogs as his sole means of haulage. This expedition achieved very little in the exploratory sense, for their ship *Endurance* was caught in the pack ice, crushed and sunk before the men had a chance of setting foot on the Continent. For a while the men camped on the pack ice, then took to the lifeboats, and nearly a year later reached Elephant Island, from where Shackleton and five of his men embarked on an 800-mile journey in the *James Caird* to South Georgia. From here Shackleton was able to organise a rescue party for the rest of his men. This epic journey is often referred to as the last and greatest of the 'Heroic Age'. Under Shackleton's unique leadership, every man survived. The dogs were not so fortunate.

The development of aircraft opened up new opportunities for exploration deep into the Antarctic. In 1928 and 1933 Admiral Byrd led two expeditions from the United States to the Bay of Whales; he landed with aircraft, track vehicles and over 100 well trained dogs with experienced dog drivers to found 'Little America' base on the floating shelf ice near where Amundsen had wintered 20 years earlier. Under Lawrence Gould and Norman Vaughan some splendid exploratory sledge journeys were made, and the first ever airmail letter was dropped to a field party by Admiral Byrd on his record-breaking flight over the South Pole.

In 1934 John Rymill led the British Graham Land Expedition (BGLE) to map the west coast of the Antarctic Peninsula. The party comprised nine men, five of whom had learnt their dog driving techniques from the Inuit Eskimos of East Greenland in the 1931 British Arctic Air Route Expedition (BAARE), led by Gino Watkins. They brought 50 dogs, a stout survey boat, a light tractor and a light aircraft, and they spent two winters on the Peninsula living largely 'off the land' – killing seals, of which there were plenty, for food for themselves and their dogs. Measured in terms of exploration achieved against cost it was probably the most successful expedition ever to sail south. Equally significant, it was the expedition's doctor, Surgeon Commander Ted Bingham, who went on to set a pattern and standard of safe and efficient dog-driving for what eventually became the British Antarctic Survey.

On board the *Terra Nova*, 1911. Captain Titus Oates with Siberian huskies and Manchurian ponies.

Looking aft on the dangerously overloaded deck of Captain Scott's *Terra Nova*, 1911. On the way south one dog was swept overboard, and back again, in heavy seas.

Patience Camp, built on an ice floe after Shackleton's ship, *Endurance*, was crushed in the pack ice of the Weddell Sea. Sadly, when the ice broke up and the men took to the lifeboats, all the dogs had to be put down.

The southern base of the British Graham Land Expedition on the Debenham Islands in the spring of 1936. Dogs were tethered outside. Only the bitches in season were given secure accommodation on the roof of the lean-to extension.        *(Photo: Alfred Stephenson)*

# CHAPTER THREE
# ANTARCTICA AND THE PENINSULA

*'It was a place never intended for life. It was as a planet somewhere in the coldness of space might be before it felt the warming energy of the sun. It was a lonely place – a place where even death is absent, for there is nothing to die; at least nothing born of this forbidding land . . .'*
Ken Pawson, Admiralty Bay, 1947/49

As late as the 1930s very little was known about Antarctica. In fact it was not until the British Graham Land Expedition that it was proved conclusively that the Antarctic Peninsula was in fact a peninsula and not simply a large group of islands. Survey work by a number of nations over many years has since proved that the Continent is a land mass about the size of Australia, almost all of which lies within the area known as the Antarctic Circle. The land mass is covered by an ice sheet that, at the Pole itself, is about 10,000 feet thick, thinning as it spreads northwards. At the point where it reaches the sea and begins to float, it is known as shelf ice, and effectively increases the area of the Continent by a further 30% – a figure that is slowly reducing year by year.

Antarctica is a land of many contrasts where, strangely enough, very little snow falls. What snow there is, is swept around by wind and rarely melts or evaporates as it would in warmer climates. Some areas remain completely dry and free of snow – as sandy and sterile as the Sahara. In other areas the snow cover is quickly blown away, exposing surfaces that are sufficiently hard and smooth to accept wheeled aircraft. In other areas still, the snow collects so that tents or even huts are often completely buried. At high latitudes for three months of the year there is almost continuous darkness and for three months, continuous sun. It is a largely desolate and inhospitable place – indeed, the coldest on earth, with temperatures reaching as low as -80°C. Virtually nothing grows here, and men must haul their stores of food with them, or

seek out the sea-borne wildlife that rest upon its rocky shores. For this reason, even today the Continent remains largely unexplored by ground parties.

The 1,000-mile-long Peninsula that protrudes northwards is utterly different in its climate, ice conditions and land forms from the rest of the Continent; and it is here that the majority of work of the British Antarctic Survey has taken place. It is an area of great beauty, with mountains rising steeply out of the sea – the highest Mount Jackson at 8,600 feet – and steep-sided channels flanked by hanging glaciers. In the spring and summertime, there is also an abundance of penguins, seals and sea birds.

The glaciers that start from the Plateau flow eastwards to the Larsen Ice Shelf which forms the western boundary of the Weddell Sea. This sea is always covered with heavy pack ice – a mixture of frozen sea, drifted snow, icebergs of many shapes and sizes and bergy bits. It is here that Shackleton's ship *Endurance* was trapped and crushed in 1915.

To the east, the deep cold of the Weddell Sea, with its heavy ice cover fed from the snows of the Polar Ice Cap, competes with the relative warmth of the Bellingshausen Sea, producing conflicting weather patterns that have an enormous effect on conditions of work on the Peninsula. In some years the cold of the east predominates and the winter's sea ice refuses to break up; in other years the ice disappears very quickly. The development of a network of bases has been inextricably mixed up with these variations.

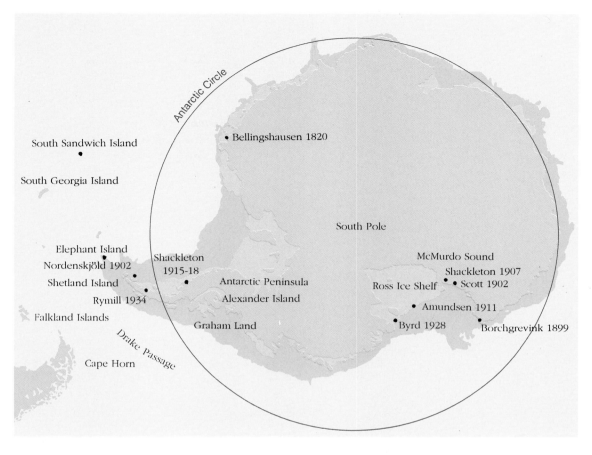

The Antarctic Continent, showing the landing points for early expeditions which included dogs.

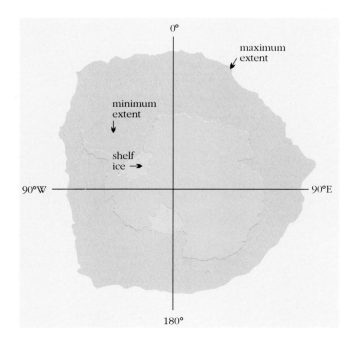

In wintertime the sea freezes around Antarctica. The extent varies from year to year, and this diagram shows the difference between 'minimum' and 'maximum' years.

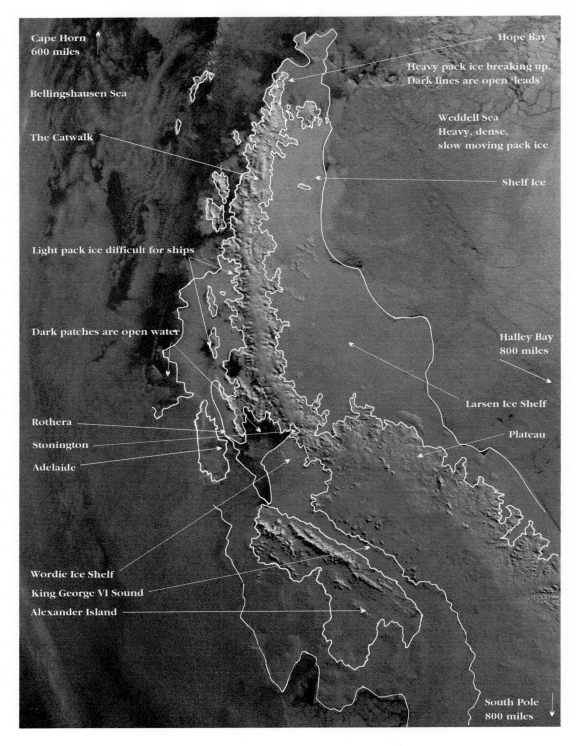

Cape Horn
600 miles

Bellingshausen Sea

The Catwalk

Light pack ice difficult for ships

Dark patches are open water

Rothera

Stonington

Adelaide

Wordie Ice Shelf

King George VI Sound

Alexander Island

Hope Bay

Heavy pack ice breaking up.
Dark lines are open 'leads'

Weddell Sea
Heavy, dense,
slow moving pack ice

Shelf Ice

Halley Bay
800 miles

Larsen Ice Shelf

Plateau

South Pole
800 miles

(Photo: NASA)

Taken from 400 miles, this Landsat satellite photograph shows the Antarctic Peninsula in springtime, when most of the sea is covered with ice.

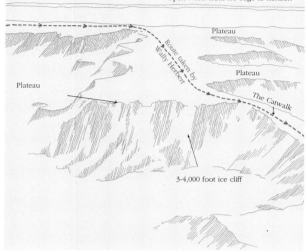

The Plateau which forms the spine of the Peninsula rarely exceeds 30 miles in width from east to west, and in some places narrows down to less than 400 yards. Distances can be very deceptive. In this picture, looking east across the Plateau, the far horizon is at least 140 miles away and there are signs of open water in the Weddell Sea. Wally Herbert crossed the Plateau at this latitude in 1957 – the only time in BAS history. The map shows the narrow neck where he had to carry his dogs rather than risk their running over the edge.

Open water from ice edge to horizon

Plateau

Plateau

Route taken by Wally Herbert

The Catwalk

Plateau

3-4,000 foot ice cliff

# CHAPTER FOUR
# THE FIRST GENERATION

*'The Eagle was the last of the Newfoundland sealers, a small wooden steamer with a clipper bow and a large barrel at her foretop. She was weak amidships and leaked for'ard . . . When she left Deception Island on 11 February 1945 she looked like an untidy Christmas Tree. On the fo'c'sle head were tethered the dogs. The deep welldeck for'ard was filled with lumber, anthracite, beds, benches, ladders and yet more dogs. On either side of the bridge a pound had been built, each heaped high with coal. Athwart the after hatch, and far too big for convenience of passage, lay the scow with lumber piled high around it and dogs inside, while aft, tied round the emergency steering wheel, were still more dogs. Four men slept aft, one on the saloon table, and the rest under the fo'c'sle head . . . None of this conformed with Board of Trade regulations but then none of the Base Leaders were official inspectors.'*

Extract from *That Frozen Land* by David James

During World War II the British made the first move towards establishing permanent representation in Antarctica. Anxious to maintain a claim on the South Atlantic, a secret naval operation, codenamed 'Tabarin', was conceived in 1943 and, early the following year, bases were set up at Port Lockroy and Deception Island to provide information on the activities of enemy and neutral vessels, known to be using the abandoned whaling stations.

With war drawing near to an end in 1945, it was decided that Britain should take the opportunity to stake her claim to parts of mainland Antarctica, too, in order that survey work begun by the British Graham Land Expedition could be consolidated and extended. For any serious travel into the Continent's interior, strong, healthy, trained dogs would be essential, and Surgeon Commander Ted Bingham and zoologist Captain N B 'Freddy' Marshall were forthwith despatched to Labrador on the north-east coast of Canada to seek them out.

In the summertime Labrador dogs lead a hard life. The snow has melted and the Inuit Eskimos leave them to fend for themselves, so that they become wild, thin and mosquito-bitten. As visits by expedition teams were well publicised it was often the case that the best dogs were 'out of town'; but with the help of a Moravian missionary, 25 huskies were eventually found and purchased. These were brought in secret to quarantine in England, and then on to the Falklands where they were picked up by the SS *Eagle* for onward passage to Antarctica. The journey from England of some 7,000 miles took 48 days, with dogs and men contending with violent extremes of weather, chronic seasickness and treacherous minefields, not to mention the vile stench of whale meat that exploded in the heat of the tropics.

The first dogs and men were originally destined for a base at Stonington Island off the southern coast of the Peninsula, but thick pack ice prevented this and instead the *Eagle* had to land her cargo at Hope Bay on the north tip. Putting stores ashore was difficult and much of the cargo had to be landed half a mile from where it was needed, then manhandled to the base site. The ship struggled back to Deception Island to pick up a second load of cargo and returned to Hope Bay where she was almost driven ashore by a north-east gale. She lost both her anchors and was all but beached before clawing her way to the open sea to return to Port Stanley. With only one-third of their stores landed and the rest in a badly damaged ship 1,000 miles away, the men had to build their new hut, train their dogs and start work hopelessly under equipped and low on food.

It was not until the following year, when hostilities ceased and sea ice conditions permitted, that a fresh attempt could be made to establish a base at Stonington Island. Operation Tabarin officially became the 'Falkland Islands Dependencies Survey' (FIDS), administered from an office on the Falklands. Heavily armed with detailed notes and advice from Bingham, and with a brand new wooden trading schooner, the MV *Trepassey,* at their disposal, Surgeon Lieutenant Stewart 'Robbie' Slessor and Sub-Lieutenant Tom O'Sullivan were sent to Labrador to pick up a second batch of huskies. Like their predecessors, Slessor and O'Sullivan found the dogs to be 'a cowering, untrustworthy and smelly lot', although in Newfoundland, where the dogs were quarantined, the two men were bemused to hear locals describing them as 'not nearly so fierce as the ones who passed through in 1934.'

Gradually, Slessor and O'Sullivan gained the dogs' trust. They hosed them down, fed and exercised them and finally shipped them south in kennels on the foredeck of the *Trepassey.* In the tropics dogs need very little food but lots of water, and an old ship's boiler was found that fitted the ship's hold. This, when filled with water, provided an essential ballast that was needed for an otherwise very empty ship. The dogs made quite contented passengers, and there were only three casualties – one who died from a meal of old rope ends and two who gorged themselves on ship's canvas. There was a trade-off, however, for during the journey six new puppies were added to the passenger list.

These two groups formed the first generation of a dog colony that was to serve the British Antarctic Survey for the next 50 years.

*(Photo: J B Farrington, Hope Bay, 1945)*

The SS *Eagle* – at the tail end of the war the Battle of the Atlantic had taken its toll and this 50-year-old wooden sealer was the only suitable ship that could be found to brave the long journey south and work in the Antarctic pack ice.

'During the journey the *Eagle* ran into bad weather and the dogs in the hold were tossed around a fair bit. Every now and then I went down to check on them and on one occasion witnessed a particularly big wave roll a dog named "Captain" right over onto his back. In order to regain face with the rest of the pack, Captain promptly jumped to his feet and charged round beating up the other male dogs. He didn't stop until every one had rolled over on its back with its legs in the air whining in the attitude of submission – an extraordinary demonstration of "king dog" behaviour. His pride restored, he lay down in the corner for a sleep.'

*Jimmy Andrew, Hope Bay, 1945/47*

The five-month-old MV *Trepassey* in very light ice. The dog kennels can be seen on deck.

Named after a famous whaling port in Connecticut, the first base at Stonington Island was established in 1940 by the United States Antarctic Service Expedition, but had to be abandoned in 1941 when America entered the war. In that season the whole coast was ice-bound and the relief ship could draw no closer than 100 miles. To evacuate the base, the expedition's Condor aircraft had to be dangerously overloaded with the 20 Americans, and the dogs put down. Arriving at this decision must have been difficult, not least because it was quite possible that the aircraft would be unable to land near the ship and would have to return to the Island, in which case the dogs would still be needed. In the event, a timed detonation device allowed for the possibility, whilst also ensuring that the dogs' deaths were quick and painless. When the British men arrived in *Trepassey* on the morning of 24th March 1946 the place resembled the *Marie Celeste*.

. . . All around lay the rotting debris of a year's kitchen refuse. The living hut was a vast barn-like structure showing clear traces of hurried evacuation: plates were unwashed on the table, meals stood stale and uneaten, and washing-up water lay frozen in its bowl – exactly as it had been left six years before. Alongside the main sleeping quarters was the workshop; the door had been left open and a five-foot layer of clear ice covered the floor, encasing the debris that was there . . . one got the impression that there had been thoughtless visitors exploring the huts since the Americans had left.'

*Extract from* Two Years in the Antarctic *by Kevin Walton*

# CHAPTER FIVE
# THE BRITISH ANTARCTIC SURVEY

*'We had set up camp at the most southerly point of our sledge journey along the Peninsula. I was sitting outside the tent with my battery-powered radio trying to pick up a time signal. As I fiddled with the controls, watching my tired dogs grubbing out the last grains of Pemmican from the snow, I suddenly picked up a German voice giving what sounded to be a speech to a very large crowd. Judging by the applause and the cheers, what he was saying was going down very well. This freak reception was so good that for a moment I could imagine myself in the crowd, cheering and applauding with them. Then I glanced up and remembered where we were: three men and 14 dogs, utterly alone, hundreds of miles further south than anyone else in the world. It was not until many months later that I realised that the voice I had heard was Hitler's.'*

Alfred 'Steve' Stephenson, British Graham Land Expedition, 1936

At the end of a long day, tent pitched, chores done and dogs fed, Steve's modern counterpart might well expect world radio to serve him with music or football results as a matter of course, and a satellite to give him his exact position. But in 1936 there were no transistors; sledge parties fiddled with a bulky battery-operated set to pick up the time bleeps that the surveyors required for their evening star observations. A 'skip wave' sending applause and cheers half way round the world was a rare fluke, and all too soon faded into the isolation and loneliness that all come to feel in Antarctica.

In 1946 technology was a little more advanced, with two-way communication between field party and base occasionally possible. However, contact with the outside world was restricted to Morse signals to FIDS headquarters on the Falkland Islands; and it was small wonder that dogs were valued as friends as much as for their traction power.

In the days of the BGLE and the first 20 years of the Falkland Islands Dependencies Survey, field work was purely exploratory. Of what rocks was the Peninsula composed? Where were the mountains and how high were they? How extensive were the ice shelves and were they moving? Which routes were the best for travel and what was the weather like? The early geologists, geophysicists and surveyors were exploring in the true sense of the word, and their quest typified that which makes man so different from other species – the unquenchable desire to learn more about the planet on which they lived. Long and hazardous journeys were made to link by the use of survey instruments the positions of topographical features. This piecing together of the jigsaw that was the Peninsula took many years to complete.

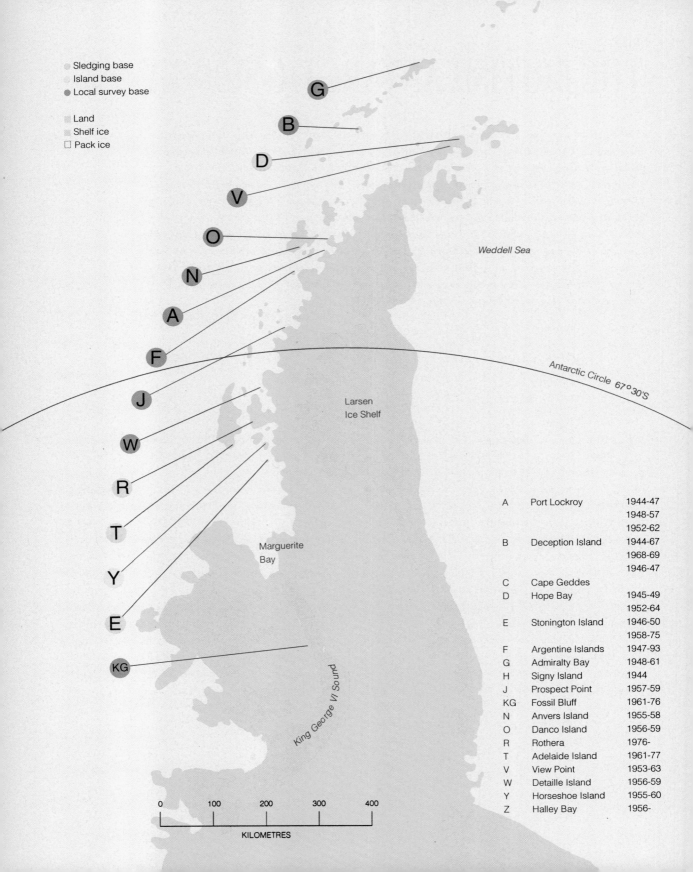

Sledging base
Island base
Local survey base

Land
Shelf ice
Pack ice

G

B

D

V

O

N

A

F

J

W

R

T

Y

E

KG

*Weddell Sea*

Antarctic Circle 67°30'S

Larsen
Ice Shelf

Marguerite
Bay

*King George VI Sound*

| A | Port Lockroy | 1944-47 |
| | | 1948-57 |
| | | 1952-62 |
| B | Deception Island | 1944-67 |
| | | 1968-69 |
| | | 1946-47 |
| C | Cape Geddes | |
| D | Hope Bay | 1945-49 |
| | | 1952-64 |
| E | Stonington Island | 1946-50 |
| | | 1958-75 |
| F | Argentine Islands | 1947-93 |
| G | Admiralty Bay | 1948-61 |
| H | Signy Island | 1944 |
| J | Prospect Point | 1957-59 |
| KG | Fossil Bluff | 1961-76 |
| N | Anvers Island | 1955-58 |
| O | Danco Island | 1956-59 |
| R | Rothera | 1976- |
| T | Adelaide Island | 1961-77 |
| V | View Point | 1953-63 |
| W | Detaille Island | 1956-59 |
| Y | Horseshoe Island | 1955-60 |
| Z | Halley Bay | 1956- |

0        100        200        300        400

KILOMETRES

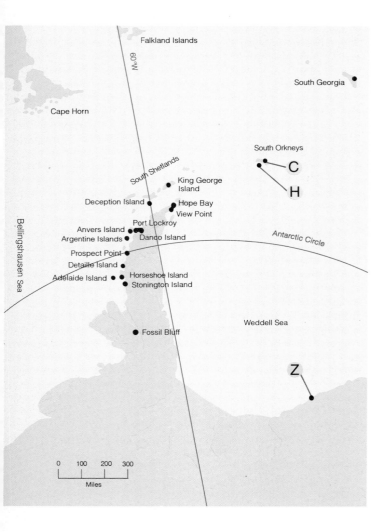

Falkland Islands

South Georgia

Cape Horn

South Orkneys

C

H

South Shetlands

King George Island

Deception Island

Hope Bay

View Point

Port Lockroy

Anvers Island

Argentine Islands

Danco Island

Antarctic Circle

Prospect Point

Detaille Island

Adelaide Island

Horseshoe Island

Stonington Island

Weddell Sea

Bellingshausen Sea

Fossil Bluff

Z

0    100   200   300

Miles

*[above & opposite]*
Between 1944 and 1976 five major British bases and 12 small bases were established, each with its own programme of earth and/or life science research to complete.

# HOPE BAY 1944 – 1964

As a base from which to travel, Hope Bay had much in its favour. Built on the mainland, travel was not dependent on the freezing of the sea ice, although journeys southward did tend to follow the coast-line. Access to the Plateau itself was made awkward by the existence of massive ice cliffs: Wally Herbert forced a route in 1957 using mountaineering techniques, but it was not until 1964, the year before the base closed, that a safe route was pioneered via Eddy Col.

Hope Bay had a chequered history. In 1948 the living hut was completely destroyed by fire, and two men died. The dogs were redistributed among various other bases and Hope Bay was temporarily closed down. Then, in 1953, the hut was rebuilt, and Hope Bay reopened to become the major base for British field work, sometimes with as many as 130 dogs on its strength.

Due to the fact that there was nowhere to build a suitable landing strip for aircraft, all journeys had to be self supported, requiring very heavy loads to establish advance depots and much duplication of effort. By far the longest and perhaps most significant journey took place in 1947: a 600-mile trek to Stonington Island, made by four men and three seven-dog teams, which provided the first complete survey link between the north and south ends of the Peninsula. It was the first one-way journey ever made in Antarctica.

By 1964 all the field work in the area had been completed and some 80 dogs were redistributed among other British bases and expedition parties.

Hope Bay in 1945 – the first mainland British base.
In the early days when the base was being built, the dogs ran loose, creating havoc in a nearby penguin rookery. From 1946 onwards, strict control was exercised throughout the British bases: adult dogs were to be kept tethered on spans at all times

'In summertime, when the snow melted, looking after the dogs at Hope Bay became something of a problem. The spans were permanently fixed on rock and unless the seal blubber was cleared away regularly it softened in the sun and spread in a sticky yellow layer. Eventually this would find its way onto the dogs so that their beautiful fur assumed a scaly reptilian appearance and reduced its insulating properties immensely. Most drivers would spend an hour or two clearing the spans and combing out the dogs.

Watering the dogs presented a major problem too. Fresh snow had to be dug and carried to them everyday. Eventually we collected enough "Ciment Fondue" tins that each dog had his own bowl. We soon found it necessary to weight the bowls down with stones as some of the dogs seemed to take a perverse delight in tipping them over, forcing you to remake the long journey to the nearest snow patch or melt stream. Most of the dogs urinated into their containers but we chose to think that the dogs knew what was good for them and were just recycling some of the most important chemicals.'

*Bill Tracy, Hope Bay and Stonington, 1960/61*

The puppy pens at Hope Bay, 1945.

This picture (photographer unknown), showing the Eddy Col route to the Plateau, was found in 1995 in the archives of Faraday Base on the Argentine Islands. The route was so steep that men had to go ahead with the aid of ice axes and crampons. Once ropes had been fixed, the men at the top could haul the dogs and equipment using muscle power.

Bills Gulch, New Years day, 1947.
On the Hope Bay to Stonington journey, the incoming party of four men and 21 dogs made a rendezvous with six Stonington men and 26 dogs who were to guide them over the Plateau.

*(Photo: Kevin Walton, Stonington, 1945/48)*

*(Photo: Julian Taylor, Hope Bay, 1954/55)*

Sledging out of Hope Bay.

The site where the first hut was burnt down can be identified just above the second pair of dogs and near the sea.

# STONINGTON ISLAND 1945 – 1975

The base at Stonington Island had the reputation for being the most difficult to access and the most often abandoned because of variations in sea ice conditions. About 300 yards long, Stonington was unique among the islands on the west coast of the Peninsula in that up until the 1980s it still had access to the Plateau via a steep 100-yard wide ice ramp leading to the North-East Glacier. This Glacier, some ten miles long, provided an effective airfield until the base was finally closed in 1975. At its head, a treacherous 3,000 foot climb led to the Plateau itself and beyond that, the East Coast. Officially named Sodabread Slope, this climb was more commonly known as 'Sodomy Slope' to those who were familiar with the difficulties of its ascent and descent.

The presence of the Glacier dominated the lives of those based at Stonington Island. The steep ice falls where it led off the Plateau, combined with the wide and relatively level expanse of the Glacier, generated the katabatic winds that blew up without warning and often lasted for days. They were nicknamed 'Fumigators' in polite company, 'Fornicators' in less; and to be caught out with a tent badly pitched, could be, and indeed was on occasions, fatal. Even on the island itself, leaving the hut for routine visits to check the dogs, or to the 'met' screen to take readings, could be hazardous. The winds played havoc with the Glacier surface: wide crevasses were often bridged and invisible, and the snow was blown into hard, corrugated iron-like ridges known as sastrugi.

There was little room for tethering as many as 150 dogs on the Island; and seeing to their needs, particularly in the early autumn before the sea had frozen, was almost a full time job. As weather conditions became more severe and the winter's snow arrived, attempts were made to provide the dogs with crude kennels but these were spurned, the dogs choosing to sit and sleep on top of them where they had a better view of all that was going on around them.

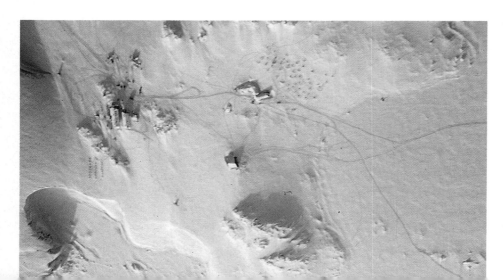

Taken in early spring 1947, this aerial view of Stonington Island shows the British base at the centre of the picture. The dots to the right are some 50 dogs on tethers. To the left are the American huts and to the left of that, the ice ramp to the North-East Glacier.

*(Photo: Kevin Walton, Stonington, 1945/48)*

(Photo: Roger Scott, Stonington, 1972/75)

Stonington Island showing the route to the Plateau via 'Sodomy Slope'.

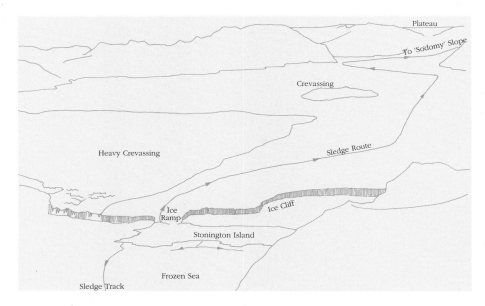

*[opposite]* Though the mountain Roman IV apparently dominates the Stonington huts, it is actually four miles away, across usually open water. This picture was taken in early spring when dogs were working in the field.

(Photo: Ben Hodges, Stonington, 1961/64)

Camped on the Plateau at
the head of the North-East
Glacier.

*(Photo: Dave Singleton,
Stonington, 1972/74)*

The 'farthest south' camp in 1947 on the east coast of the
Peninsula, 600 miles from 'home'.

That year the Americans had returned to Stonington
under Finn Ronne and reoccupied their base huts. Finn
Ronne had taken advantage of the enormous quantities of
American military equipment now declared 'surplus' and
brought with him three aircraft, four tracked amphibious
vehicles known as Weasels; and all the cold weather
clothing and rations that he could load onto his ship. His
party comprised 21 men and two women – the first to
winter in Antarctica – and 30 huskies. Sadly, many of the
dogs died from distemper on the voyage south, and this
led to the British and Americans combining forces – the
British lending their dogs, the Americans lending their
aircraft – for fieldwork, including a joint survey of the east
coast of the Peninsula. 'Darkie', driven by Dougie Mason,
led from the front for the whole distance – 1,200 miles in
89 days. This was the first fully air-supported field journey
undertaken in Antarctica and was not to be repeated for
another 12 years.

*(Photo: Bill Latady, member of the Ronne Antarctic Research Expedition)*

John Tonkin with pup 'Simon', late summer 1947.

'In dog wars it was men who were the peacemakers and in an odd sort of way in man wars
it was the dogs who were the peacemakers. The 1960/61 season saw four of us living
closely in one room of the iced up Stonington hut. The resulting pressures of living in such
close proximity are obvious. I can remember well how one of my colleagues used to clean
his plate with his finger after each meal and how, completely unreasonably, this would
make me squirm. The saving grace for this stress of close relationships and lack of privacy
was undoubtedly the dogs. One would emerge from the hut in an Antarctic winter twilight
to the welcoming chorus of barking and howling. Perhaps they were expecting another
meal – but no, they had only just been fed. The realisation would dawn that the general
excitement was for you and you alone, and already the tensions and frustrations of base life
were beginning to lift.'

*Peter Forster, Stonington, 1957/61*

*(Photo: Kevin Walton, Stonington, 1945/48)*

Stonington Island in 1974.                                          *(Photo: Jim Bishop, Fossil Bluff, 1972/75)*

*(Photo: Ben Hodges, Stonington, 1990)*

A close-up view of Stonington Island in 1990. Fifty years has seen a great deal of change: the ramp to the North-East Glacier has gone for good, and the Glacier itself is broken up and impassable. Stonington is now a real island, and the only visitors to its collection of lonely and abandoned huts are tourist ships.

# THE ANTARCTIC TREATY

Towards the end of the 1950s, major changes were taking place in the world's perception of Antarctica. The last continent to be discovered, Antarctica has no indigenous inhabitants to lay claim upon it and there was a growing realisation that this unique status should not be destroyed by nations carving it up into 'slices of pie'. In an attempt to contain the damage and to prevent the commercial exploitation of resources, 1959 saw the signing of the Antarctic Treaty by the 12 countries which had participated in the Antarctic research of the International Geophysical Year 1957/58. The Treaty took effect on 23rd June 1961. From this point on the Continent was to 'belong' to no-one. Rather it was to be viewed as an international scientific laboratory where all nations were equally welcome and whose findings could be shared by all. The Treaty has since been signed by a further 14 countries, with 13 others agreeing to abide by its terms.

Shortly after the initial signing, the Falkland Islands Dependencies Survey changed its name to the British Antarctic Survey, administered from offices in London and Cambridge, and slowly the scientific work began to change in character. Basic geological, geophysical and topographic mapping continued throughout the 1960s, but on the Continent itself the relatively new science of glaciology spread its wings: the mapping and measuring of the enormous heat sink of ice. Radio echo systems were developed whereby the thickness of the ice could be measured by radio signals transmitted from aircraft, bounced off the bedrock and received back into the aircraft again. Detailed maps of the sub-ice surface were produced that in truth posed more questions than they answered, not merely about the constitution of Antarctica but that of the whole planet. Whilst aircraft support and track vehicles were developing apace throughout this era, the safest form of surface travel continued to be a sledge drawn by well trained huskies.

# HALLEY BAY 1956 –

Halley Bay was built in 1956 as part of Britain's contribution to the International Geophysical Year. A high level scientific research station manned by members of the Royal Society, it was not built on land, but upon 1,000-foot thick shelf ice that rose and fell with the tide of the Weddell Sea beneath it. From seaward the edge of the ice formed an unbroken vertical cliff some 100 feet high.

Initially, all research took place at the station itself; but it was then discovered to be lying in an area of intense auroral activity, and when the Geophysical Year came to an end, the British Antarctic Survey

was asked to continue with ionospheric, geomagnetic and auroral studies, as well as initiating field work in the mountains some 300 miles inland. So it was that dogs came to Halley Bay.

Scenically, the base had little to commend it: miles and miles of featureless snowscape, the northern aspect broken only by the tops of tall icebergs trapped in the ice of the Weddell Sea. Situated just 1,000 miles from the Pole, the winter nights at Halley were long and dark, with the sun making no appearance at all for two whole months in midwinter. The build up of snow was much greater than at the Peninsula bases, the temperatures much lower, and high winds causing everything to become buried in drift snow – including the huts, so that access had to be made via entrance tunnels and ventilation shafts. The subterranean troglodyte existence made severe demands on those who were based there.

Due to the severity of the weather, Halley Bay had the distinction of being the only base where dogs were housed underground in wintertime. The 'dog tunnel' was begun in 1968 as a simple trench dug into the snow and roofed over; but as this required the men to climb up onto the snow surface and then down the trench in order to see to the dogs, the arrangement soon seemed impractical. Harry Wiggans, one of the men stationed at the base that year, then had the idea of digging a 30-foot vertical shaft, tunnelling 100 feet into the hard glacier ice, and giving direct access to the base hut so that going 'outside' would be unnecessary.

Travel from Halley also had its share of complications. Between the base station and the mountains 300 miles away, lay the dreaded 'Hinge Zone', a vast area of chaotic crevassing where the land-based ice sheet was continuously grinding its way outward to become shelf ice floating on the sea. Distances travelled in a single season often exceeded 2,000 miles, and gave rise to unique methods of travel, combining dogs and machines in a sort of relay race. On dangerous terrain, particularly in crevassed areas, the dog teams would go first to establish a route. Once the dogs reached safe ground the vehicles would lead, with dogs pulling light loads in their tracks, or riding as passengers in custom-built pens on a cargo sledge.

The RRS *Bransfield* moored at the edge of the shelf ice. The base was four miles inland.   *(Photo: Dave Fletcher)*

The typical view that greets visitors to Halley Bay – radio masts and a London Underground sign indicating the entrance to the base hut buried beneath the snow surface.

*(Photo: Dave Fletcher)*

'The dog tunnel at Halley was pretty unique, and its existence brought in a whole new range of dog-manoeuvring techniques, as well as a vastly increased use of four letter words. Once the surface temperature neared -50°C, the whole base would get involved in what was known as "Balls Over Day". Redecorating the underground kennels for their new occupants was a simple matter of scraping the walls with a spade. A tripod would then be erected over the shaft, together with a pulley and block, and the dogs placed one by one in a harness and flicked "balls over" as they were lowered down. This disorientated them so that before they knew what had happened they were safe and sound at the bottom. Trying to get dogs past already-occupied kennels could be difficult, and the noise quite deafening. The dogs would at last settle to feed; while the worn out men retreated into their own hut. It was pretty claustrophobic in the tunnel, but no dogs were lost to the climate and, provided the kennels were kept clean, they emerged none the worse for wear – just extremely anxious to air some pretty mean grievances with their next door neighbours!'                                    *Dave Fletcher, Halley, 1978*

*(Photo: Peter Clarkson, Halley, 1968/75)*

'The dog-carrying Maudheim sledge was a typical example of FIDS innovation in response to the logistical problem of the terrain and distances involved in travel from Halley. Two 45-gallon oil drums were placed at the front of the sledge and two up-turned Nansen sledges without handlebars formed the sides. These were secured to the Maudheim by lashing, with the tarpaulin wrapped over the tops of the Nansens. We were concerned that the dogs would react adversely to being in such close contact, and certainly on the trial run they seemed edgy. However, when it came to the real thing, they became quite enthusiastic about it, evidently realising that this was an easy way to travel. Not stupid those dogs.'

*Graham Smith, Halley, 1967*

Dogs in transit to the Therons, Spring 1967. In this case the 'kennels' were simply mounted on a tractor sledge.

*(Photo: Colin Wornham, Halley, 1966/67)*

'Although strenuous efforts were made to keep the dogs away from penguins, things weren't always so simple. At Halley Bay, the situation was more difficult because the penguins weren't the small 14-inch Adélies, they were your full blown three-foot Emperors. One day, sledging across the low shelf to the east of Halley, we came across a group of penguins, and "Helix", a very young dog, slipped his harness and made a beeline for them. One of the large adults stood his ground and, at the moment of impact, caught Helix's head neatly between his flippers; he rattled it about like a football until Helix's eyes were spinning round and he staggered backwards – only to receive a sharp peck on the nose. Helix beat a hasty retreat, whilst the penguin preened himself, then tobogganed off in a leisurely fashion.'

*Dave Fletcher, Halley, 1978*

# ADELAIDE ISLAND 1961 – 1977

As a Peninsula base, Stonington Island had many shortcomings and by 1961 it was apparent that a new location was required. Though lacking in picturesque qualities, Adelaide Island some 70 miles to the north-west was to serve the British Antarctic Survey well for the next 15 years. The airstrip became the centre for all air operations and remained so until Rothera was established in 1976/77. Prior to 1968, planes arrived in the Antarctic by ship and were assembled and wintered at Deception Island where there was an aircraft hanger and an airstrip of sorts on a cinder beach. In 1968 the purchase of the first Twin Otter changed this procedure: its size and range meant that it could fly direct from South America to Adelaide Island.

Many a dog team and field party spent the winter at Adelaide and then, if and when the sea ice permitted, travelled over to Stonington to join the spring exodus of teams heading out for the summer field season. Alternatively, it was not uncommon for a complete team of huskies, together with a laden sledge, to be loaded into the aircraft so that they could be whisked quickly and painlessly over impassable terrain to locations which would have been impossible to reach a few years earlier: an hour or so's flight and the bemused dogs would be unloaded to start a season's field work fresh.

The mid-1970s saw further changes in the approach to scientific research. Radio-echo studies showed that 85% of all the world's fresh water was frozen into the Antarctic Continent, and it was universally recognised that this ice sheet held a unique record of past climates. Slowly the keys to unlock the secrets of the ice were discovered, and it became apparent that the behaviour of this enormous freezer had a direct effect on the climate of most of the Southern Hemisphere. As the geological patterns of the Peninsula began to make exciting sense, so geologists with specialist interests requested to spend whole seasons at specific locations. The need for unsupported overland travel decreased, and with it the role of the huskies.

When Stonington closed in 1975 the remaining 50 dogs were brought to Adelaide and the following year, when that base closed too, they were moved on to the new base at Rothera Point. The main reason for the move was the rapid deterioration of Adelaide's runway and ice ramp. Increasingly warm temperatures and, to a certain extent, pollution had caused crevasses to appear in both, rendering the facility unsafe for use in the latter part of the summer.

# ROTHERA 1976 –

Built on a rocky peninsula sticking out from the south-east corner of Adelaide Island, and with an ice ramp accessing a sizeable snow field for an 'all-weather' aircraft landing strip, Rothera is now the only occupied British base on the Antarctic Peninsula. Its setting must surpass that of all the other bases. It is almost surrounded by beautiful mountains rising directly from the sea, and from their lofty heights tumble glaciers and icefalls beyond compare. On a clear day it is possible to see the mountains of Alexander Island some 100 miles south across Marguerite Bay. The base is ideally situated for access to the fjords that offer some of the most interesting sledging of the Peninsula.

The purist might argue that Rothera was never a sledge dog base and it is true that the base's primary role has been to support field parties using Skidoos rather than dogs. However, for the 18 years between 1975 and 1994, dogs were an integral part of base life and some impressive 'recreational' journeys and mileages were recorded.

Rothera Point.
Dogs were kept on the north-west corner of Rothera Point, well out of the way of the busy comings and goings. It was the job of the General Field Assistant to look after them, but most of the men and women liked to have some involvement with the dogs.

*(Photo: Simon Gill, Rothera and Halley, 1986/92)*

'Here, "Nuk" is keeping an interested eye on what is going on in the sledge store workshop. Only one or two of the dogs did not enjoy being indoors; most adored the attention and fascinating surroundings. Nuk could be lulled into giving us a howl; "Pris" would follow your every move like the most loyal pet; "Mouse" invariably forgot himself and made a puddle on the floor; whilst old hands like "Blackie" would enjoy the warmth, sprawl out and receive a tummy rub. All usually found the odd stray morsel of food lying somewhere forgotten.'

*Brian Hull, Rothera, 1990/92*

One of the last recreational runs, Rothera, 1992.

*(Photo: Ben Osborne, Rothera, 1989/92)*

# CHAPTER SIX
# FOLLOW THAT DOG

*'Seldom elsewhere have I heard such foul language as is used by a dog driver. Whatever stories a driver may tell you, he never has 100% control over his team — only degrees of lack of control.'*

Angus Erskine, Detaille, 1956/58

All travel in Antarctica involves considerable danger. There is sea-ice to break through, crevasses to fall into, avalanches to be buried under, and blizzards to get lost in. The proper use of well trained dog teams provided a safety factor that made almost all of the early exploration of the Continent possible – and where British field work was concerned, that meant dogs leading out in front.

Of the men who first went south as part of the Falkland Islands Dependencies Survey, only Ted Bingham, base leader at Stonington Island, had any previous experience of driving dogs. The others, recruited for a combination of their specific skills and all-round abilities, initially saw dog driving as a means to an end. They were soon to discover it was a skill in which to take pride and from which to draw pleasure every bit as much as the scientific work for which they were being paid. Bingham taught them that in order to accomplish safe and efficient travel, the organisation of the team was all-important: accordingly it had to be specially tailored to suit the nature of Antarctic field work where vast distances, featureless horizons and heavily crevassed terrain would so often be the order of the day.

On many of the early polar expeditions, a man had walked ahead of the dogs, leading the way and warning of oncoming dangers; but Bingham recognised that this method presented additional dangers of its own. Firstly, if the surface were hard and smooth the man would have to run – pursued, and often overtaken, by a team of enthusiastic huskies.

Secondly, with a man ahead, it is more difficult to maintain accurate direction than with a dog-led team steered by command on a compass bearing. And thirdly, perhaps most importantly, if the area ahead is crevassed the man must be tied to the sledge by a safety rope. A rope dragging in the snow would worry the dogs, whilst walking ahead with no rope was an unjustifiable risk. Better a dog down a crevasse than a man; better still, neither. Thus it became a 'rule' that dogs should always lead in front, and that men should not be allowed out in the field until they had proved they could drive them from behind. This rule imposed a discipline that was hard to adhere to, for whilst huskies love to pull, few will take the initiative and lead with nothing to follow. Over the years, however, the rule was to minimise disaster and maximise achievement.

Dogs are naturally both gregarious and competitive animals and quickly establish a hierarchy among the packs they form. Bingham, as others had before and after him, soon learned to observe this hierarchy and to exploit the dogs' different personalities in the arranging of a team. Teams were usually run in formations of either seven or nine, the general principle being brains at the front, brawn at the rear. Partly because of this, the best leaders tend to be female: more sensitive, more alert and less inclined to fight. Harnessed behind, the stronger dogs are content to chase after them all day! Alternatively, one dog might hold a grudge against another and will spend his days trying to catch him in order to air the grievance. Almost always a 'king dog' would also emerge, one who, perhaps because of age or size, would boss the other dogs and keep them in order. Another dog might take the role of cheer leader – forever anxious to be underway and able to galvanise the others into action. But invariably it was the lead dogs who became the heroes of the stories. They were the ones who had to set the pace and keep the team strung out; they chose the safe route through the crevasse field, gave warning of thin ice and, perhaps most importantly, responded to the commands of their driver and made it possible for him to control the team by word of mouth from the relative safety at the rear of the sledge.

Because these were Eskimo huskies, efforts were made to retain the commands they recognised – 'Auk' meaning right, 'Irra' left, 'Up, dog,' to get ready, 'Huit' to go, and 'Ahhh' to stop. Learning the words was easy: learning how to express them so that the dogs would respond to them, was not. Most 'Fids' have memories of inheriting their first dog team, and finding themselves incapable of achieving anything with them. The result is a rather depressing sit-down strike by some confused huskies. In the process of trying to move them, the driver shouts himself hoarse and exhausts himself pushing his own sledge. Alternatively, if the driver has not asserted his position as 'king dog' he may find a full scale dog war erupting before him.

Robbie Slessor having a discussion with 'Darkie'. Trained by Ted Bingham, 'Darkie' was the very first team leader at Stonington. He was a ruffian of a dog to look at, with a torn ear, and must have seen a lot of fighting in his youth. But it soon became apparent that he had excellent eyesight, was very sensitive and very, very intelligent. Once he was trained to Bingham's satisfaction, it was relatively easy to use him to teach other leaders. He set a remarkably high standard for them to follow.  In 1949 Vivian Fuchs, later to become Director of FIDS/BAS, inherited him as a team leader. He wrote in his journal that year:

'It was interesting to observe Darkie's technique when he sensed danger. He advanced cautiously, somewhat in the fashion of an heraldic lion or leopard, each paw extended as far as possible to test the surface in front of him. In this way he found every crevasse and successfully crossed the majority, whereas those behind went blundering into them in spite of the obvious holes he had made. Others would suddenly dash sideways to avoid an imaginary crevasse which was no more than a surface marking in the snow, which Darkie had ignored. Indeed with him ahead, be it on glacier or thin sea ice, I can move forward with the greatest confidence . . .'

*(Photo: Kevin Walton, Stonington, 1945/48)*

Equally difficult once 'on the road', was learning just how much encouragement to give the dogs. If the driver was continuously shouting at them, they either became winded trying too hard, or they began to ignore his rantings and ravings so that when that extra bit of effort was required it became difficult to achieve.

The driver's other fear was, of course, to have the team run off without him. Watching a team disappear into the great white yonder, together with sledge and all essential items required for survival, is at best embarrassing and at worst dangerous. To reduce the risk, many tricks had to be learnt: for instance, never leaving the sledge to walk back along the trail, and making use of a short length of rope affectionately known as the 'dongler'; one end of this rope would be attached to a waist belt, the other looped over the handle bar upright. Another precaution was to trail a long rope, with a large knot on the end, from the rear of the sledge, the idea being that the driver could make a dive for this if the dogs took off unexpectedly – always a last resort as he might well find himself dragged along in the snow for a mile or so before they came to rest.

The reality behind good training was months, if not years, of blood, sweat and tears in the field, with driver and dogs gaining confidence in each other, learning to exploit and accommodate their respective strengths and weaknesses, and adapting techniques to travel in varying terrain. With a good diet and careful breeding, the result was a team that could pull a heavy load up hill and down hill; through deep snow, slush and water; over complex crevasse fields, glare ice and sea ice; in sun or blizzard; and for eight or more hours a day.

'Captain, I soon learned, was the king dog of my team, and I found him far more capable of imposing discipline than I was. When trouble arose and some dog or dogs got out of line he would charge at the ring leader, hitting him with his chest and knocking him off his feet. He would then stand over the cowering culprit, growling until that dog submitted – which usually occurred at once, but if not was quickly dealt with by an encouraging bite. As his strength and teeth deteriorated Captain utilised the services of a black thug of a dog called "Scotty", whom he had browbeaten as a pup. Between them order was quickly restored and authority regained. Scotty never seemed to realise how he was being used and enjoyed the prestige. He was still firmly under Captain's thumb – or paw – when I left the Base.'

*Jimmy Andrew, Hope Bay, 1945/47*

'Captain' in retirement at Admiralty Bay, teaching a bunch of pups some of his old tricks.

*(Photo: Ken Pawson, Admiralty Bay, 1947/49)*

'"Nanok", the oldest dog in my team, was as tough as nails and a regular old soldier. He had broken his leg some years before and he would show you his operation scar when you asked him. He ran with a bitch called "Mary" just behind "Joe", the leader. In actual fact he was a much stronger personality than Joe but just didn't like to run out on his own; it was months before I realised that part of Joe's apparent stupidity when he was supposed to be breaking trail and not deviating from a set course, was really Nanok doing some successful back-seat driving.'

*David Dalgliesh, Stonington, 1948/50*

Kevin Walton with the Orange Bastards team on training run.

'Under Ted Bingham's guidance, I chose "Rover" as my lead dog and took him out regularly with "Darkie" so that he became familiar with the sound of the commands and what they meant. Learning to steer a compass course was a vital stage in the training procedure: while shouting "Irra" (left), I would flick a 40 foot whip out a few feet to his right, and this made him instinctively veer to the left. With care and constant practice he learnt to hold that course with only occasional prompting for miles and hours on end.'

*Kevin Walton, Stonington, 1945/48*

'The whip was made of a long thong of walrus hide, with a short and supple butt end. When I first tried to use it, the tail end wrapped itself around my head and gave me a black eye. So I lashed the butt to a broom handle and next time I swung it well away from me at arm's length. I guess that I was more afraid of the whip than the dogs were, for I never tried to hit them with it after that. In time, the whip was phased out altogether, and the "thumper" brought in. This was a short length of one-inch manila rope with a back splice in one end and an eye splice in the other. Hit against the sledge it made a frightening noise, which quickly brought the dogs up short, and was altogether much easier to use!'

*Gwion Davies, Hope Bay, 1944/45*

'Driving a team in white-out conditions is difficult. On this occasion we were up on the Plateau and desperately short of food. We knew exactly where we were, that the terrain was crevasse-free, and that a food depot was 15 miles away, so we set off to look for it. Four hours later, the bicycle wheel milometer trailing behind the sledge told us that we had gone the distance and we set up camp to wait until visibility improved. I only hoped the months of training Rover to hold his course had paid off. They had. A day later the weather cleared to reveal that we were only 100 yards from the depot.'

*Kevin Walton, Stonington, 1945/48*

'I arrived at Adelaide in 1974 at the tender age of 21. I was probably a little too arrogant for some people's liking and definitely very vulnerable to the merciless banter and leg-pulling skilfully practised by the "Fids" in residence there.

Ian Henderson, a self-assured, lively character from the wilds of Northumberland suggested that I help him feed the dogs. Ian had spent the previous two and a half years sledging with the dogs and obviously considered himself to be an old hand. I had happened to mention to him that I was keen to do some dog sledging and probably implied I thought there would be nothing to mastering the techniques required.

Feeding the dogs was apparently a messy business and so we dressed up in Ventile outer garments that were used for no other purpose; they were so impregnated with rancid seal blubber they would have competed with the best oilskins. Once dressed we collected the harnesses and set off for the dog spans where the sledge we used for seal carcasses had become half-buried in drifted snow.

The dogs were frantically running round in circles on their chains by this time, knowing full well it was feeding time. Ian showed me how to lay out the traces and prepare the sledge, casually suggesting that we would need nine dogs to pull the fully loaded sledge back up from the seal pile. This seemed a little excessive, I thought. We quickly harnessed up the dogs and then clipped them into their respective places on the gang line. They were facing the ice ramp towards the air strip, and, above the noise of the dogs, Ian shouted to "run the dogs up it before turning them so as to take the wind out of their sails before coming down to base." He told me the commands, then released the anchor and the dogs took off at full pelt up the hill, with me holding on for dear life.

Suddenly, to my horror, lead dog "Sue" changed her mind about where she wanted to go and turned the team towards base. Our speed increased as we started to descend. The small braking device on the back of the sledge proved totally ineffective on the hard icy surface of the ramp. I began screaming at the dogs, begging them to slow down. This only seemed to make them go faster. Unfortunately for me they also veered one hundred yards or so left of the course we had walked up. Ahead of me now, instead of the gradual slope of the ramp, there was an ice cliff dropping some ten feet to the sea shore below. The dogs were going too fast to do anything except jump off the edge. They landed surprisingly gracefully. The same could not be said for me or the sledge as we hit the stones below with an almighty crash. Amazingly I managed to hold on to the sledge as the dogs continued running as if nothing had happened. Ahead of us, strategically placed, lay numerous empty oil drums. The dogs negotiated a course between them; the sledge however bounced off one to the next, creating a noise similar to war drums in darkest Africa. Emerging on the other side of the drums the cause of all the urgency was plain to see. The seal pile! A considerable number of partially decomposed seal carcasses lay piled up

between the walls of a rocky gully. Once amongst the seals the dogs had no desire to leave but my troubles were far from over. As is unfortunately the way with huskies, they became most uncivilised when it came to sharing food and began to fight. By the time I had gathered my wits together, all nine dogs were engaged in deadly combat. I lay into the dogs in a futile attempt to disentangle them, only to find myself becoming plastered in putrid seal flesh.

A feeling of frustration and embarrassment overwhelmed me as I noticed that most of the base members had assembled above me on either side of the gully. They were all having a good laugh at my expense. I had been well and truly set up. They all knew the outcome of my attempts to feed the dogs was likely to produce some first class entertainment and were occupying the ringside seats. My ego had been totally deflated.'

*Rick Atkinson, Adelaide and Rothera, 1975/78*

Rick Atkinson with 'Yvonne' of the Picts.

'I will never forget my first experiences with the dogs. Oliver "Dickie" Burd, the departing base leader, gave me a quick run down on them – too many names to remember – and then was gone. With our ship still in harbour we were enjoying a cup of tea when we heard an almighty fight break out. Confident in our instruction that huskies would not bite a man intentionally we waded in bare-handed. The statement was reasonably correct – if in error a jaw closed on something that was not dog, the owner would quickly release it with an "Honestly, I didn't mean to" look on its face.

That evening we held a post-mortem and decided that the dogs were testing the water with the new base team. A few days later, after carefully reading the "How to Drive a Dog Team" notes, four of us decided to give it a go. Harnessing a dog was described as a "one man job" – not for us. As soon as we appeared with a bunch of harnesses, all hell broke loose. It took two of us to get the harness on and just one second for the dog to slip it off. And as soon as our backs were turned, they were off again for a friendly scrap. It took a full hour to get them ready to go.'

*David Golton, Argentine Islands, 1947/49*

'Once during the winter I took my dogs out on training run on a circular route and came back across the lake. A recent gale had blown most of the snow away and the bare ice was so slippery that the dogs could hardly keep their feet. I was keen to get back to the hut for supper. I had a pair of crampons in the sledge bag so I put them on my boots and finding they gripped the ice well I took a trace and started to pull the sledge alongside my dogs. The dogs continued to slither around until "Joanna", a cunning one, thought "To hell with this," and jumped onto the sledge where she sat looking smug. The other dogs followed her example until I was pulling the lot of them. I crept past the hut, hoping no one would look out of the window and notice, but no such luck – my colleagues have never allowed me to forget it.'

*Angus Erskine, Detaille, 1956/58*

Artist unknown. This cartoon was discovered in the Faraday base archives, 1995.

'Cape Lachman, on the Prince Gustav Channel side of James Ross Island, was an area where seals often congregate and sunbathe, and inevitably we came across many blow holes. It was pandemonium when a seal shot up into the middle of a dog team – a fierce rugby scrum of seal, rope, dogs and sledge, all mixed up. It was hell at the time – though it seems funny now. The seal would often slip out long before the dogs noticed and then my job of untangling started. It's a wonder we weren't heard in the Falklands.'

*Noel Downham, Hope Bay and Stonington, 1961/64*

'In a land almost devoid of life there are few things that hold the gaze and attention of the dogs like a seal that has hauled itself onto the sea ice. To the left of this picture a crabeater seal was basking in the sun a few feet from its blow hole. The dogs were aware of its presence for a mile or two before they could see it. Their ears prick up, their pace quickens and their tails rise. The ill-disciplined team will become single-minded about the direction in which they want to head. There was always an element of risk associated with seal encounters as a bite from a seal could transmit a severe infection.'

*Rick Atkinson, Adelaide and Rothera, 1975/78*

Finding one's way following old dog tracks marked by pillars of yellow ice and dark dog droppings was known as 'Shit and Piss navigation'.

*(Photo: Brian Hull, Rothera, 1990/92)*

'There was no fixed rule for pup training. At nine months of age the pups were large enough to be put in harness and taken on short runs pulling an empty sledge. They were generally introduced into the main team between one year and 18 months old, sometimes one at a time to run beside an old campaigner who ensured the pup minded his manners, and sometimes as a pair. If the pups had been well used to human contact, they would generally work from the word go. Those that didn't, more often than not turned out to be reluctant workers for the rest of their days.'

*Simon Gill, Rothera and Halley, 1986/92*

Eight-month-old 'Spike' and 'Monty' – exhausted after their first official field trip.

# CHAPTER SEVEN

# HITCHES, HARNESSES & SLEDGES

*'At one spot we stopped for photographs and were just starting off again when seven dogs and trace but no sledge shot past Brian and myself. Looking back we saw Geoff Hattersley-Smith and Dan Jardine with the sledge and the two remaining dogs. Apparently "Mac", one of their team, and a devil for biting his trace, had spent the time while we were stopped, chewing through the main trace, the result being that when the "Huit!" was given and the dogs pulled, the rope snapped and most of the team got away. We had to travel a mile or two before we caught them.'*

Ken Pawson, Admiralty Bay, 1947/49

## HITCHES

There is no 'right' system for hitching a dog team to the main hauling trace of a sledge. There are basically three ways and each has its staunch supporters.

The 'centre trace' (see diagram 1a overleaf) comprises a long central rope to which short links of thinner rope are attached picking up the harness rings of individual dogs. The shorter the individual link the less freedom the dog has to pick his own route but the less distance there is to fall if a crevasse bridge collapses beneath him. Against that, he is more likely to be pulled down if the dogs ahead of him break through.

With the 'modified fan' (see diagram 2a), an adaptation of the Inuit Eskimos' 'fan', the dogs run in pairs, but each one is hitched on a separate trace, and is free to take his own track – particularly useful if he wants to 'lift a leg'. The other advantage of this system is that in the event of a dog falling down a crevasse, he will not drag others down with him. The disadvantage is a greater chance of fights breaking out.

A combination of the two systems has all dogs on a centre trace but with much longer individual links (see diagram 3a). This provides more freedom and less risk of the dogs being dragged down a crevasse.

In the early days all main traces were linked to the sledge using three-strand, natural fibre rope with a large, easily handled wooden toggle. Individual links were made from ¾-inch hemp rope, impregnated with Stockholm tar to discourage the dogs from chewing. In the case of the centre trace, the short links were spliced to the central rope. Later on, the heavy central rope had steel rings spliced in at intervals and the separate links were looped into these rings; this meant that they could be adjusted and changed according to the particular driver, and the whole shortened or lengthened at will. As they became available, natural fibres were replaced by man-made fibres which proved stronger – and, sadly from the dog's point of view, less chewable!

Dog team running
on centre trace.

*(Photo: Gordon McCallum,
Adelaide, 1962/63)*

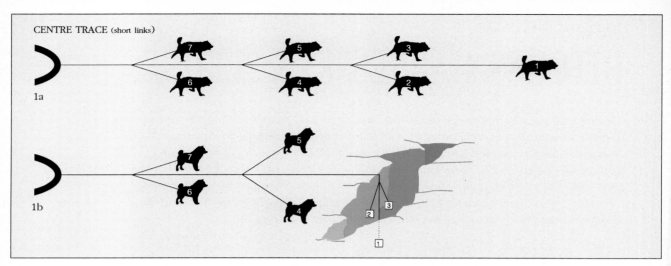

CENTRE TRACE (short links)

1a

1b

FAN TRACE

2a

2b

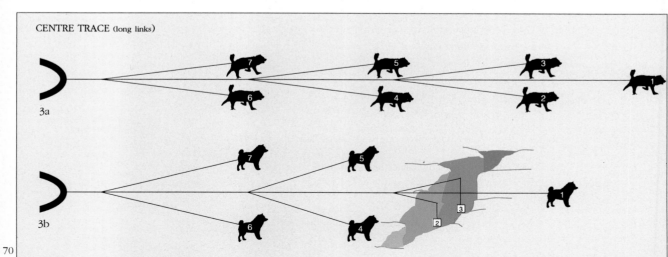

CENTRE TRACE (long links)

3a

3b

'You can tell that the surface is fast and the sledge running well, as only half of the traces are tight and the dogs are trotting. The front seven dogs, apart from the one on the left who has temporarily broken rank, are harnessed by a fan trace. The last two dogs are so-placed because they are apt to be lazy and only work under supervision.'

*John Killingbeck, Deception and Adelaide, 1961/62*

*[opposite]*

Controlling a dog team on centre trace with short links is relatively easy as long as there is a good leader who keeps its trace tight. This system is useful for puppy training: as one of the back pair, the puppy soon learns that it is easier to run and pull than be dragged through the snow on its bottom. However, if the leader breaks through an unseen crevasse, as in Diagram 1b, the odds are that its weight will drag down the dogs that follow. Rescuing three dogs, all on one rope, will be difficult.

The modified 'fan' works well only with a well disciplined team, due to the length of the individual links. If a dog falls down an unseen crevasse, as in Diagram 2b, each casualty is on its own trace and rescue should be a relatively easy operation.

In Diagram 3b the leader has managed to cross an unseen crevasse, but the second pair have not been so lucky. No one dog has pulled another down, and rescue should, again, be straightforward.

# HARNESSES

The dog harnesses used by FIDS/BAS were of simple design that changed little over the years. They were made from lampwick, the tubular cotton webbing used in oil lamps, which always stayed reasonably soft, even when frozen. This material was available long before nylon webbing had been invented and in many ways it was more suitable. The harness design essentially followed what is still considered the most effective way of distributing the load onto the dogs, most of the pressure being taken by the breast plate of the chest, leaving the shoulders to move freely and the windpipe free from pressure. The simplicity of design did not, by any stretch of the imagination, achieve the desirable transfer of load along the line of the spine and invariably the dogs ended up pulling somewhat crab-fashion. Rather like an old fashioned back pack, it did the job but more comfortable designs are now available. The main advantage of this simple construction was the ease with which the size could be altered, allowing them to be kept fitting snugly, and preventing escape, which could prove disastrous in crevassed areas. For the escape 'artists' among the team, and also to help prevent dogs falling out of the harness while hanging in a crevasse, a small loop and toggle could be sewn into the leg loops to improve security.

Each dog's harness was individually made by the driver, with the dog's name sewn onto it – an occupation that whiled away the long winter evenings!

Gordon McCallum harnessing 'Ossian' of the Giants team.

'To remove the harness the dog is gripped between your knees and each paw pushed through the loops. Usually the dog is quite helpful whilst the operation is carried out but some can be awkward; they sit there with adoration in their eyes, head on one side and, carried away by the personal attention they are receiving, forget to bend their legs. Meanwhile you are becoming colder and colder, dreaming of the warm tent and the cup of tea you know to be waiting.

Another engaging habit some of the dogs have, especially if they have done a good mileage, is to nibble at your hand – their paws being a little tender they are trying to tell you to be gentle with them. Others think it is time to play and lie on their backs waiting for tummies to be tickled, making it almost impossible to remove the harness.'

*Bill Tracy, Hope Bay and Stonington, 1960/61*

'All husky dogs coveted the art, few ever managed it: that art was the ability to slip their collars. "Flush" of the Komats team was a veritable Houdini, and no amount of precautionary measures ever fooled her. Once she absconded from the night-span on a local sea ice trip out of Stonington and trotted off into the fading gloom of mid-winter twilight before any one could catch her. Twenty-four hours later she was discovered sitting patiently at the base hut door. No one knew where her escapade had taken her but her return route must have crossed difficult sea ice and an erratically calving glacier snout.'

*Geoff Renner, Stonington, 1964*

'The base hut at Stonington had a lean-to extension which was used exclusively for dog gear. It was kept moderately tidy with a row of wall hooks, each belonging to a particular team. On the peg was hung the driver's whip and the traces belonging to his team. With them was a set of used dog harnesses and probably a brand new spare set ready for some future journey. The bundles of harnesses were gay to look at as each was marked with its own combination of brightly coloured tabs as well as the dog's name. Above all, there was the strange doggy smell, a queer mixture of sweaty harnesses and seal oil, crushed puppy meal, tarred rope and much used leather collars.'

*Extract from* Two Years in the Antarctic *by Kevin Walton*

# THE NANSEN SLEDGE

Adapted by Fridtjof Nansen from various Eskimo designs, the wide-runnered sledge that bears his name has proven to be remarkably effective. It was used almost exclusively by FIDS/BAS field parties for nearly 50 years and in that time required only minor improvements.

Built with selected, aircraft grade, sawn ash, the sledge was light, flexible and resilient, and could carry 1,000+ lbs over rough terrain. It was 12 feet long, with four-inch wide runners that curved up at both ends. This meant that they could be pulled backwards to get out of trouble as easily as they could move forwards in normal use. They were also reversible – handlebars could be switched so that back became front if front runners were damaged. Held apart by five bridges, the runners, were covered with a smooth, resin-based laminate to reduce friction, and later with low friction,

high density plastic. Handlebars at the rear gave the driver something to hang on to, and there was also a foot-operated brake. In later models, drop down steel plates were used to reduce sideslip on a traverse, and an emergency brake, in the form of a heavy rope which dropped under the runners, was held clear with a simple slip lashing. A semi-circular bamboo 'cowcatcher' acted as a buffer in the event that the sledge overrode the dogs.

The dogs were attached to the sledge with a rope bridle that was spliced onto the base of the middle bridge and then wrapped around the second and first bridges. Behind the sledge trailed a bicycle wheel fitted with a milometer – this method of measuring distance was employed during the British Graham Land Expedition, and remained in use until the advent of Skidoos with built-in milometers.

The loaded Nansen Sledge.

(Photo: John Noble, Stonington, 1966/67)

*(Photo: Ian McMorrin, Stonington, 1962/64)*

Sledges were assembled on base from British materials. Each took a good 40 hours to build and required regular maintenance. They tended to be rebuilt every season and broken parts replaced, although some were known to last intact for several years. The workshop in this picture was in fact the original ten-man living hut, built in 1945.

At Hope Bay in summertime all snow disappeared around base and dogs often preferred to lie on sledges rather than hard stones. In this case they are using a very solid and heavy Greenland Komatik sledge, previously used by the 1952 British North Greenland expedition.

*(Photo: Hugh Simpson, Hope Bay, 1955/57)*

'During the first half-mile dash of a morning each dog's digestive system would get moving. Young dogs who had not yet mastered the art of crapping on the run were dragged along by the rest of the team, desperately trying to maintain a squatting position. They tend to give each other's crap a wide berth, and the driver too would take immediate action to avoid it, pulling the sledge off to one side by edging both sledge runner and his own skis. Collision, however, was sometimes unavoidable. The turd disappeared under a runner where it froze and stuck, impairing the glide efficiency and slowing the sledge like barnacles on a boat's hull. There was no easy way to remove frozen turdicles; if your sledging companion was not too far away you could call a halt and together turn the loaded sledge on its side. The alternative was to unload the whole sledge, scrape the runner and reload. One such episode was bad; it was infuriating when you ran bang smack into another black mess within minutes of getting under way again.'

*Nick Cox, Rothera, 1979/81*

*[opposite]* The Admirals team setting out for a trip from Stork Mountain, near Rothera Point, February 1992.

*(Photo: Dr David Wynn-Williams)*

# CHAPTER EIGHT
# A DOG'S DINNER

*'On sledging trips there really wasn't much difference between dog food and man food. The Dog Pemmican was coarser than ours, but it tasted good, and it was an evil temptation to eat it with our own 1¾ lb daily food ration. We restrained ourselves as we knew the dogs earned every crumb of their whacks. If we caught a seal we cut it up into 14 parts, one for each dog in the two teams, and kept the head for ourselves. That sharing of food brought us together in comradeship, dogs and men.'*

Gwion Davies, Hope Bay, 1944/45

Provided with suitable and ample food, huskies will willingly demonstrate their capacity for sustained physical exertion under the most trying of conditions. Neglect this fundamental requirement and the consequences will soon become apparent. They are generally intelligent animals but when food is available they have been known to eat to the point of death, and when it is not available, they may equally work to the point of dropping.

It is generally agreed that the Antarctic husky required about 3,000 calories per day for maintenance and between 3,500 and 6,000 calories when working. Variations depended on the prevailing conditions (more calories being required when pulling heavy loads up hill in low temperatures) and on the size of the dogs.

Dogs are carnivores and require a fairly regular supply of meat. While at base, and occasionally in the field, the dogs were fed from the ample seal population – one four- to six-lb lump, including bones, every other day. Fresh or frozen solid (they devoured it happily either way), seal meat was found to keep them in excellent health. The blubber, too, was easily digested, and provided a source of concentrated calories when needed, particularly in the winter months. Seal meat with blubber provides around 2,000 kcal/lb; lean meat only around 500 kcal/lb. Three-quarters water, seal meat also provided a considerable amount of the dogs' water requirement.

The dogs were always well fed prior to departing on field journeys and were partly sustained by their own body fat when working – a 'feast and famine' existence not far removed from how the wolf lives in its natural environment. Back at base they rapidly regained any weight loss and displayed no ill effects. One of the Antarctic huskies' most redeeming qualities was just how little food they required when you consider how hard they worked and how cold it was.

In the very early days field rations were provided in the form of dried stockfish; this was hard and wood-like, but when soaked could make a nourishing and palatable meal for humans as well as dogs. In the 1930s and 40s, explorers took with them compressed 1 lb blocks of dried ground beef and beef fat known as 'Man Pemmican' and 'Dog Pemmican' – not unlike large OXO cubes. Gradually fish meal, milk powder and ground maize were added to the dog recipe now referred to as 'Old Nutrican'. This was found to be unsatisfactory and was superseded by 'New Nutrican' – or 'Nutty' – from 1958 onwards. Consisting of beef fat, whale meat and corn flakes in equal proportions, with a calorific value of about 2,500 kcal, it remained the standard fare of every nation's Antarctic huskies.

Both Pemmican and Nutrican are extraordinarily long lasting: field depots of dog food over 40 years old have been recovered and found to be in perfect condition.

It was normal practice to feed each dog one block of Nutrican per night, and an extra one every third night if it could be spared. This ration did not provide the dogs with their full calorific requirement but to feed more on extended expeditions would have been impractical. To make up the shortfall, wherever possible the dog driver would supplement the diet with seal and feed extra blocks to the dogs when at a depot.

The performance of dogs, as of men, was monitored regularly in Antarctica and extensive dietary improvements were made over the 50 years, most notably by medical officer Neil Orr; but only recently has the suggestion been made that their performance may have suffered from dehydration. The dogs tended not to drink water when it was offered to them, and it was always assumed that they acquired sufficient water by eating snow. This was probably true in terms of survival, but not in terms of optimum health. When travelling on hard packed snow, for instance, the dogs had difficulty rasping up more than a few ice crystals; and on the spans at base, the urine-soaked ice must have been even less appetising. Unlike humans, dogs sweat only through the pads in their feet, but the water loss through eight hours' hard labour in the cold, dry climate of Antarctica was considerable. Dehydration may also have exacerbated such problems as fighting, chewing, perhaps even infertility.

That then is an account of the official menu, but ask a driver what his dogs eat and the answer he will probably give is 'Practically anything!'

Feeding time – 1990s self service style.

'Usually we threw the meat to the dogs, but John Sweeny thought it would be more fun to let them help themselves from the Pulka (a 40-gallon drum cut in half). Being creatures of habit, it was amazing to watch them looking repeatedly from the lumps of meat to you, waiting for their piece to be thrown. But most got the hang of things pretty quickly. One dog named "Wendy" was noticeably very fussy and took her time sniffing and choosing. It was easy to imagine her being a pernickety housewife looking for the best value cut in the butcher's shop.'
*Brian Hull, Rothera, 1990/92*

"'Joey", like most of the puppies, was allowed to run free around the hut and one night he disappeared. We searched but could find no trace of him and after a couple of days gave him up as lost, assuming he had got onto a piece of loose ice and been carried out to sea. A week later, Geoff Hattersley-Smith and I were out climbing on Flagstaff Peak, some 700 feet above base level, and came across Joey, his head stuck inside a 24-lb bean tin. He was trying to back out of the tin – indeed, as the evidence before our eyes suggested, had been for some time and distance. Very carefully we eased the tin – in which we found two smaller tins – off his head and the well-remembered furry face emerged, none the worst for having been enclosed for so long. Joey followed us back to base, quite happy but very hungry. He must have found the tin on the waste dump near the hut, and got stuck in the process of trying to lick it out. In future we flattened large empty tins before putting them on the dump, so nothing like this could happen again.

*Ken Pawson, Admiralty Bay, 1947/49*

*(Photo: Michael Skidmore, Halley, 1967/69).*

'To conserve the seal population we had been sent mutton. It was an experiment in dog food we had been told – an appeasement to the influential nature lovers – the preservers of Antarctic wild-life who consider the ration of three seals to one husky for winter dog food an unjustifiable slaughter. But the dogs began to show symptoms of scurvy. Their hair fell out and suppurating sores developed; they stuck to the ice in pools of their urine and tore off flesh if they jumped up too suddenly. The rifle shots were strangely muffled that ended the lives of those poor creatures, and we dragged their bodies to the pressure ridges to be chewed up by the grinding ice.'

*Extract from* A World Of Men *by Wally Herbert*

Dismembering a fresh seal in the field.

*(Photo: Gordon McCallum, Adelaide, 1962/63)*

*(Photo: Geoff Renner, Stonington, 1964),*

'On one trip we took along a book called *Man Meets Dog* by Konrad Lorentz, the animal behaviourist. One of his suggestions for keeping dogs in line was to mimic the bullying actions of the big dogs. It sounded logical enough and the dogs being an unruly bunch I was anxious to put it into practice. I watched them for a while and noticed how the big dogs took hold of smaller ones by the ears and shook them. It seemed to work effectively enough so I tried it out on "Princess". Never again! Remembering too late that dogs are copraphagic – they eat each other's faeces – I came away with a mouthful. It would appear that "Jet" had earlier had a snack around Princess's rear end, before trotting round to the front to indulge in a bit of courting. Re-cycled Nutrican isn't tasty and I don't recommend it.'

*Noel Downham, Hope Bay and Stonington, 1961/64*

'A standard 20 man-day sledging food box contained 7 lbs of butter in 1 lb tins for a high protein/high calorie diet. There was much competition among the dogs for who would be allowed to lick out the tin, the fight resembling a rugby scrum.'     *Peter Forster, Stonington, 1957/61*

'One morning "Mac" of the Terrors team picked up a discarded tin of rancid butter and carried it all day in spite of the determined attempts by the rest of the team to trick him into dropping it. Come evening, he settled down to enjoy it, crunching it up so that the butter squirted out through the tooth holes in the metal.'     *Dave Matthews, Signy and Stonington, 1964/66*

'We had adopted the practice of taking sandwiches with us for the first lunch of our sledge journeys. Being a bit of a squirrel I often kept one back to eat a day or two later as a change from the hard biscuit and Pemmican which formed our routine diet. Both dogs and men would gaze at me enviously. One day, taking a break whilst out sledging, I laid the precious sandwich on top of my mug of hot cocoa to thaw it out a bit. "Sidney", who was running loose because of ice balls in his feet, saw what I had done and crept towards me. I knew he was there but was distracted momentarily. He chose that split second to leap forward and grab the sandwich. I realised what was happening and hurled myself on top of him, grabbing it out of his mouth before he could gulp it down and stuffed it into my own. Somehow it didn't taste quite as good as it should have done but there was no way I was going to let Sidney have it.'     *Jimmy Andrew, Hope Bay, 1945/47*

'There were only two pups reared at Adelaide my first winter there, "Giles" and his sister "Yvonne". They became the focus of much attention and were allowed all sorts of privileges. One day I brought them a fleshy seal rib; it measured about 14 inches long – the pups weren't much longer than that – and I presumed they would play tug of war with it. Not a chance. Giles, who later in life became famous for his brawn rather than for his brain, snatched the rib from me and swallowed it down whole. I couldn't believe my eyes. How that tiny body managed to accommodate the rib defied all logic.

Well, the days went by and there was no sign of ill effects, save perhaps a little stiffening in the way he walked. His appetite in no way diminished and he was just as lively as ever. Then, ten days later, Giles was chasing his sister at full pelt across the slippery vinyl floor of the mess hall when, in full flight, he let out an almighty squeal. I turned my head in time to see the cause of what must have been intense pain in Giles' backside, be jettisoned across the hall with remarkable force. The little pup regained his composure instantly and resumed the pursuit of his sister as if nothing had happened.'

*Rick Atkinson, Adelaide and Rothera, 1975/78*

'At Hope Bay we had to gather seals whenever the sea ice in the bay seemed safe enough to sledge on. Leopard seals are aggressive animals and can move very fast. On this occasion we needed the food and took a chance to get close enough to kill him. He was huge but, to our disappointment, his flesh was almost impalatable, even to the dogs.'

*Vic Russell, Hope Bay, 1945/47*

'On one occasion we had three teams pulling in line ahead. A dog in the leading team found a six-inch length of nylon cord as we left camp and swallowed it. Later that day the cord emerged from his rear end and was gulped by a dog in the second team. Later again it was discharged and seized upon by a dog in the third team but this time it had a knot in it and the dog spat it out. Odd sensibilities!'

Angus Erskine, Detaille, 1956/58

'It tastes so much better chilled.'                    (Photo: John Noble, Stonington, 1966/67)
'Perky' of the Vikings team.

# CHAPTER NINE
# SLEDGING WITH DOGS

*'Sometimes the mists would close in and bleach even the faintest shadows below the dogs' bellies. They would seem to be running on nothing more solid than the heavy stagnant mists we disturbed in our passage. The motion of sledging on those occasions gave the illusion that the dogs were a ghost team that ran without moving, and the sledge sliding and squeaking over a soft cushion of snow was but part of a dream through which we were living.'*

Extract from *A World Of Men* by Wally Herbert

Sledging with dogs is a unique experience, forever offering new sights, sounds and sensations. Everyone who worked with the British Antarctic Survey has his memories of dog sledging days: it was then that the sheer size, starkness, loneliness and beauty of the Continent became vividly apparent. There were days of drama, days of danger, and days of downright misery and discomfort. Days when the dogs behaved and days when they didn't, their antics as endearing as they were frustrating. There were days of great tragedy and days of sheer delight when conditions were perfect and everything seemed to go right.

The enthusiasm of the dogs, their hunger to travel, to be always on the move whatever the conditions, was insatiable. It was also infectious, and on many occasions the dogs pulled not only sledges, but men's spirits, spurring them on to discover what lay beyond.

The Giants team passing in front of Mount Liotard, taken from the sea ice off Ryder Glacier.

*(Photo: Alan Wright, Adelaide, 1961/63)*

'There is nothing quite like the semi-chaotic and exhilarating take off at the beginning of the day. One ski off, one ski on, trying to avoid last night's pool of frozen dog pee. The dogs were always eager to be on the move, barking, straining at their harnesses, their patience stretched to the limit. When the anchor was knocked away, the dogs would leave at a sprint. In all but the worst snow conditions the driver had to cling on to the back of the sledge for dear life or be pulled along on his skis. It was essential to make immediate voice contact with the lead dog, if only to set off in the right direction.'

*Nick Cox, Rothera, 1979/81*

*(Photo: Roger Scott, Stonington, 1972/75)*

In deep soft snow no dog team could be expected to break a new trail and pull a loaded sledge, but there are no known crevasses here so the driver has gone ahead to encourage them.

'Driving a team where mountains or icebergs lie ahead provides few problems, but if the terrain is flat, open snowfield to the horizon the dogs will soon lose interest in working. Drivers have different ways of overcoming this. Personally I found whistling or singing produced remarkably increased performance. Although it is easier and more efficient than singing, whistling for hours into the teeth of a cold wind is quite difficult. Fortunately dogs are friendly, if undiscerning critics, always ready to overlook wrong notes or a raucous voice, and romp along with renewed vigour. For me "Onward Christian Soldiers" always called forth their best efforts, perhaps because it was one of the only two tunes which I can roughly reproduce. The other is "Show me the way to go home".'   ***Extract from*** Of Ice and Men ***by Sir Vivian Fuchs***

'Over fifty days after leaving base, we were on our way home. Three nights and two days of gale had held us down, giving us the lie-up we needed after a week's hard running. Now we were ready to move on. That morning the wind had dropped, tent canvas no longer flapped, drifting snow was stilled, and the sun shone warmly through the peak of the tent. We emerged to a glorious day – calm, clear and brilliant.

Alert to our movements, the dogs rose as we did, popping up from the snowdrifts that had built up around them, stretching, yawning, shaking ice from their matted fur, greeting us with warmth and wagging tails. They watched as we dug out tents, boxes, sledges and traces, growling *sotto voce* to each other, from time to time setting up the chorus of song that bonded them as a community – three teams of nine, offering friendship without question to the four men who moved among them. Harnessing brought them to a crescendo of excitement. As the first team moved off, those remaining leapt in their traces. I had often wished I could raise even half their blessed enthusiasm at the start of the hard day's sledging.

My team was the Choristers, a nickname earned by their penchant for bursting into song. From time to time I sang to them, and during the ten-minute breaks they sang to me and to each other. I sang Hymns Ancient and Modern, Handel, Gilbert and Sullivan, Schubert, and a Bing Crosby-Andrews Sisters medley. They sang a chorus much older and more mysterious – half mournful, half joyful, and wholly memorable to all who heard it. "Nero", the leader, and "Nigger", his second in command, were respectively baritone and *basso profundo*. "Judy", the lead bitch who ran with them, was a *mezzo*, with all the makings of a convincing Carmen – particularly when on heat. "Raven" and "Crow", identical twins, were reedy tenors: "Jackdaw" and "Mouse" were counter-tenors with a heart-searing upper register. Bringing up the rear were "Mutt" and "Jeff", two young dogs with uncertain voices: they had auditioned well for the team and shown promise. At full belt the Choristers could have given a good account of themselves in any chapel north of the Trent or west of the Severn.

We caught up with the leaders, enjoying lunchtime break off a group of low-lying islets, uncharted and unrecorded in mid-fjord. The dogs found snow to roll in, then slept blissfully in the sun. The wind had dropped: we could munch our biscuits stripped to the waist, and indeed roll tentatively in the snow ourselves. Ken Blaiklock took a quick sunsight and plane-table survey, Spiv and David knocked rocks for the geological collection and I searched for biological specimens.

After a two-hour break the dogs were bored and ready to go. I led off, crossing a field of frozen-in brash ice. Here we came upon Adélie penguins, all trotting eastward in groups of six to a dozen toward their breeding grounds along the coast. To Nero, Nigger and Judy the penguins represented original sin – diversions irresistible, to be pursued if only for a few happy yards before traces and the sledge stopped. Three times the trio whooped off like hounds after hares, followed closely by six delinquent team-mates and more distantly by myself and a cavorting sledge. Three times their roistering jammed the sledge hard between bergy bits. Immobilised, they howled abuse at the penguins while I howled abuse at them, and the team following closed up to join in the fun.

We sledged over 20 miles that day, doing a worthwhile job of discovery and survey in perfect weather and idyllic surroundings. In the evening we camped by another unrecorded islet, spanning the dogs on fresh snow, rewarding them and ourselves with a feed of seal-meat. One of the bitches surprised us by producing two healthy pups, which the four of us fussed over and settled in a nursery – my spare pullover – alongside their mother.

We perched comfortably on boxes outside the tents, celebrating the happy occasion with brandy from the medical bag and enjoying the evening calm. As the shadows lengthened across the sea ice, the Choristers found cause to celebrate. "Hallelu-u-ja," they sang to the setting sun; "Hallelu-u-ja" chimed in 18 other huskies – and so did we.'

*Bernard Stonehouse, Stonington, 1947/49*

Enjoying an evening wash in the Skidmore Valley. Geoff Lovegrove with 'Skye' of the Hairybreeks team.

*(Photo: Colin Wornham, Halley, 1967)*

*(Photo: Rod Pashley, Adelaide, 1969/70)*

'Rob Davies had been having a bad day. We were travelling across deep, soft snow – never easy – and from my vantage point in the following sledge I watched as his dogs drove him to distraction with their uncooperative behaviour. One dog in particular seemed more in the mood for play than work, and eventually Rob was forced to stop the sledge altogether and give him a good talking to. As always, the dogs' timing was immaculate; with a concerted effort all nine lunged forward, dragging the sledge behind them and knocking Rob off his feet. In fear of losing them, Rob managed to grab hold of the sledge as it was passing over him and hung on for all his worth. Some considerable distance further on his team ground to a halt – more likely due to lack of ambition than from the muffled cries coming from under the sledge. I could see that the soft snow and heavy sledge load were making it impossible for Rob to extract himself; so, with tears of laughter running down my face, I pulled up my sledge and gave him a helping hand.

*Rick Atkinson, Adelaide and Rothera, 1975/78*

In an attempt to keep two teams travelling at about the same speed, the lead sledge would be lighter in load, making it easier for the dogs to break trail. Under these conditions the dogs would pull their loads at about four miles per hour.

'This was our second day out from the base and all the dogs are dirty after spending the winter on the spans. The team is travelling through well formed sastrugi caused by sustained periods of strong winds, and the nose of the sledge frequently gets caught under the lip of a ridge, bringing sledge and dogs to an abrupt halt. Ahead, the depressions caused by the sunken bridges of two crevasses can be clearly seen. The dogs were naturally reluctant to cross these visible crevasses but after we had tested the bridges with a probe they were declared sound and we all crossed safely.'

*Roger Scott, Stonington, 1972/75*

'This is what every dog and man sought to avoid. Crevasses are caused by the movement of glaciers and vary enormously in width, size and depth. They are often bridged over with wind-blown snow or fresh snow which, in good conditions, can be detected by undulations in the snow surface. In bad conditions, they are hard to detect at all. We often practised extracting ourselves from these gaping, perilous voids, but this did little to ease the anxiety they caused. The experience of lowering oneself down is humbling: it is as if you have entered the gates of another world, the icy blue stillness at once threatening and overwhelmingly beautiful. Death never seemed far away, and the thought of having one's corpse preserved intact for all time is little consolation.'

*Rick Atkinson, Adelaide and Rothera, 1975/78*

*(Photo: Ben Hodges, Stonington, 1961/64)*

'Sodomy Slope' – a pause for a breather on the final haul.

(Photo: Ben Hodges)

'Sodomy Slope' from the top of the Butson Ridge.
The steepest part is at the bottom and in 1946 all loads were hauled up using a long rope. That year, when the dogs were only part-trained, it took six men with three teams nearly a month to get two tons of load to the depot. Extensive crevassing flanked the route, and it was not until the base was reopened in 1958, when lack of sea ice made other routes south impossible, that further attempts were made to climb this treacherous slope again.

(Photo: Peter Forster, Stonington, 1957/61)

Taking one's team from the Plateau down to the North-East Glacier was exhilarating but could prove disastrous. The relatively flat Plateau changed to a slope of about 1 in 4 in a matter of yards. After 600 yards if one failed to stop in time, and turn right onto the traverse, the snow slope led straight over a vertical 2,000-foot ice cliff.

    At the end of a long journey the loads were relatively light but the dogs had realised that this was part of the last run home and all too easily preferred to cut corners if given half a chance. To add further excitement a belt of crevasses lay on the left hand side of the traverse. The last sledge to go down without load from the top was always popular, as the track would be well worn and fast.

'We were nearing the end of a four-month, 1,000-mile sledge trip, and one final hurdle awaited us – the terrifying 3,000 foot descent of "Sodomy Slope". Though the ascent had taken us ten long days at the beginning of the trip, the descent would, in theory, take only half an hour. Visibility was poor that day and Mike Fleet, myself and the two other teams took a break to discuss the whereabouts of the survey pole we had left to mark the only safe route down. We finally agreed on the direction and I called "Pull away, dogs!" My team, the Moomins, surged forward, out of my control, and for a moment I feared that we might plunge over the glacier; then I realised that the lead dog had spotted the survey pole: she was heading for home. A long drawn out "Aaahh now" brought them under control and we came to a halt at the top of the descent.

Controlling our rate of descent was a major problem and we wrapped as many chains and ropes as we could around the sledge runners to try to prevent them from over-running the dogs. I put "Harvey" and "Eccles", the strongest and slowest dogs, on a long trace and fastened them to each side of the sledge to provide extra braking power. With a cry of "Up Dogs! Huit!" my team and I began the terrifying descent, the two other teams following behind at five-minute intervals. The rushing nightmare lasted for two long minutes before the brakes took any noticeable effect and we began to slow down.

We had nearly reached the end of the traverse when "Dot", my lead dog, quite suddenly vanished. The pair behind her also disappeared, and it was then I saw the faint line of the crevasse. The other three pairs of dogs dropped from view in quick succession. Mike and I hurled our combined weight to one side and managed to overturn the sledge. A painful jerk, as the falling dogs reached the end of the traces, dragged the sledge a couple of feet nearer the hole before it ground to a halt. My worst nightmare had been realised: my entire team – my friends and fellow travellers – all lost in one go.

I crept to the edge of the hole and looked down. It was a horrible sight: the dogs were swinging helplessly, some 30 feet down a bottomless pit, and howling with fear. I returned to the sledge, found some rope and, with shaking hands, put my crampons on. Ron Tindal and his team arrived, lashed their sledge to ours and spiked them to the ice. Secured by ropes, I was lowered down into the crevasse. The dogs were quiet now and I soon reached the first two hanging a few feet below the lip. The other men sent down another rope and the first two dogs were quickly hauled to the surface. My heart sank as I saw that the next two harnesses, belonging to "Aramis" and Eccles, were empty: they had wriggled free only to fall to their deaths.

The next four dogs were taken out as smoothly as the first two and I lowered myself still further to reach the last dog, Dot. Just as I fixed her to the rope, I saw, far below me and perched precariously on a small "ice island", Aramis and Eccles. It was a miracle. They were alive.

Aramis was quite easy to send up, although I had problems with the heavy and strangely-shaped Eccles. I was soon exhausted and were it not for the strength of the men at the top I would never have been able to haul myself back. The rescue had taken over an hour.

The last 14 miles back to the safety and comfort of base were made as we had set out four months ago – as a full team, with the dogs pulling willingly and strongly.'

*Ben Hodges, Stonington, 1961/64*

Sledging on the Plateau.

*(Photo: Peter Forster, Stonington, 1957/61)*

*[opposite]*
A similar but less dramatic crevasse rescue.

*(Photo: Rod Pashley, Adelaide, 1969/70)*

(Photo: Roger Scott,
Stonington, 1972/75)

Tragically, the year after their escapade on 'Sodomy Slope', the whole Moomins team was killed, along with the Trogs team and their drivers, Tom Allan and John Noel, on the North-East Glacier. Tom, a diesel mechanic, and John, a radio operator, both competent mountaineers, left Stonington Island with the dogs on 24th May 1966. Their trip had been planned as a 'Jolly' – a reward for being cooped up at base for the season – but 24 hours after their departure they radioed back to base that the weather was deteriorating and that they planned to dig well in. The dreaded katabatic wind known as the 'Fornicator' blew for three days, with speeds reaching an all-time record of over 100 knots. When it died down, attempts were made to contact the two men but no response was received and Neil Marsden and Keith Holmes were sent out to search for them. Marsden's diary picks up the story:

'At 1430, just as were losing the light, we reached the area where we knew they had camped, and spotted dark shapes on the snow surface. As we drew nearer, we realised that they were the bodies of John Noel and four of the dogs. 120 yards down wind, buried up to his arms in snow, stood Tom Allen; he was inadequately dressed, and an avalanche shovel lay at his side. It was a horrible spectacle; as if time itself had been frozen. We rushed back to

base; but due to more bad weather it was not until four days later that we were able to return. By this time the snow was hard and windpacked. Tom stood, as we had left him, at the entrance to a snow hole. We could only surmise what had happened. In the silence of their dug-out the two men had perhaps not appreciated the strength of the wind, nor realised the rate at which the snow was building up. Tom had probably gone out to see to the dogs, had lost his way in the driving snow and John, half dressed, had crawled to the entrance of the hole to see what he could do to guide him back. In the meantime, the dogs, still on their tethers, had literally been drowned by the build up of snow – in several cases only their rear legs and tails were visible from the surface. I could imagine Noel shouting his head off in an effort to guide Tom back to the safety of the dug-out, and, becoming colder and more tired, must have just fallen asleep and never woken up.'

Footnote: It was a tremendous example of courage that John remained where he was, ever hopeful that his companion would return. The bodies were brought back to base and buried by their comrades beneath two piles of stones. A cross stands there today in memory of them.'

'In January 1974 I was near the end of a three-month field trip on the east side of the Peninsula, with Dave Burkitt and two dog teams, his the Admirals, mine the Ladies. "Nig", one of the Ladies, was a real trollop, and had managed to slip her collar and mate with "Slioch" a month earlier. She was obviously getting near to her time, so when the aircraft from Stonington flew in to bring us more supplies and collect our rock specimens, it returned to base with one extra passenger. For Nig the flight was only the beginning of her adventure. We heard the rest of the story when we reached base a month later. After meeting the plane on the North-East Glacier, the base members returned by Skidoo-hauled sledges, Robin "Twiggy" Walker nursing Nig on his lap. Not far from base the group stopped among some crevasses to adjust loads. While this was going on, Nig wriggled free, pulled her head through her collar, and ran off, refusing to be caught. The party moved on slowly, confident that she would follow, and from some distance watched anxiously as she crossed the wider crevasses one by one. Just as she seemed to be safely over, she vanished.

Rushing back to her rescue, the men found Nig wedged 15 feet down the crevasse, and in imminent danger of drowning in the melt water which had collected at the bottom. The crevasse was so narrow that Twiggy had to have a rope tied around his ankles and be lowered down head first. Twice he got stuck, and when at last he reached Nig she was frenzied, biting his hands and arms in her panic. He finally got a hold on her, but she was too firmly wedged for him to pull her free. With the rope cutting painfully into his legs, and the blood rushing to his head, he had to be brought up again to have his wounds staunched.

Meanwhile Nig was swallowing water and weakening. None of the other men were small enough to go down and get her out, so everyone frantically shovelled snow into the hole until it formed a sufficiently large mound for Nig to rest her head upon, clear of the water. Then they lowered the rope again, hoping to lasso it around her neck, but Nig seized it between her teeth and nothing would persuade her to let go. As they cautiously exerted increasing pull on the rope, she gripped it the tighter – and quite suddenly her body came free. They continued hauling, every moment expecting her to let go and fall back into the crevasse, but she hung on grimly and soon they had her lying shakily on the surface, wet through, shocked and exhausted. Such was her attachment to the rope by this time that still no one could remove it from her mouth.

The party brought her into base on a sledge, and placed her on a blanket to dry out in front of the fire in the hut. Much cherished by everyone, she got up two hours later and walked about, very subdued but apparently unharmed. Within a few days she was once more her eager self, and the men settled down happily to await her confinement.'

*Dave Singleton, Stonington, 1972/74*

*(Photo: Rod Pashley, Adelaide, 1969/70)*

*[overleaf]*
'The North-East Glacier had to be treated with great care as the crevasses were large and often difficult to detect if the light conditions were bad. It was important to stick to a very well charted route and Mount Walton was one of the aiming marks for the first long leg.'

*Peter Forster, Stonington, 1957/60*

(Photo: Ian Sykes, Stonington, 1967/68)

Bills Gulch.

(Photo: Ben Hodges,
Stonington,
1961/64)

'Bills Gulch is a fearsome alley of jumbled ice falls and crevasses caused by Plateau ice spilling steeply towards the sea. Spend a night camping in the Gulch and you soon learn that it is a restless place. The ice speaks to you in a voice reminiscent of gunfire. Each report signifies a crevasse splitting or a serac cracking. The route through is a tortuous switchback where parties frequently lose sight of one another. Only the foolish did not fear it. We certainly did . . .

It was mid-May by the time the six-man East Coast party made their scheduled rendezvous at Three Slice Nunatak at the east end of Trail Inlet. Temperatures in the area had already been recorded down to -47°C and daylight was becoming scarce as midwinter approached. As it was still too early in the season to guarantee sea ice in Neny Fjord the return via Bills Gulch was unavoidable; a total distance of 60 miles. Nor was it made any easier by the sledge being unduly overloaded with redistributed equipment, one of the two other sledges being used to stretcher

a badly injured geologist. A few days earlier he had become victim of a white-out – the invisible landscape of polar environments. Such was its deceitfulness that it had lured two dog teams – the Trogs and the Spartans – over a 30-foot ice cliff.

In difficult terrain it was customary for the teams to close up at intervals. At 11.00 a.m. we did so but with a stunning realisation. The third sledge was missing. Man, sledge and the nine-dog complement of the Terrors had disappeared. The conclusion was immediate – they had been claimed by a crevasse. And Bills Gulch was full of them, either lurking beneath a snow cover, gaping, or broken open by a passing sledge. Cautiously retracing the route a yawning hole was found, cut into the lip of which was a severed dog trace. Duly safeguarding the dog teams the men belayed and peered over the edge – 50 feet below the motionless Kelly lay wedged between the side walls. Further down, the blueness turned to blackness but with sufficient light to distinguish irregularities in the ice. There was no barking but there was a voice – Noel Downham was shouting up that his injuries amounted to no more than a damaged thumb and bruising! His fall must have been cushioned by the thick snow bridge on which he had come to rest.

It took a full four hours to retrieve what was recoverable. The splintered sledge was irreparable. However, by far the greatest loss were two of the dogs. "Nick" had broken his back and had to be put down, whilst "Jade" died from internal injuries. Both lie buried in the crevasse with the remnants of the sledging unit. Of the surviving dogs "Jet" and "Mac" recovered from damaged legs whilst "Bryn" overcame severe shock.

At camp that night the men mourned their losses but counted their blessings. There was also time to speculate as to how anyone could survive a vertical drop of 120 feet.'

Geoff Renner, Stonington, 1964

Travelling in white-out conditions.

*(Photo: Ian Sykes, Stonington, 1967/68)*

'Towards the winter of 1973 John Yates and myself were out on a field trip on the Plateau near Stonington. Sixteen days into the trip and we had accomplished next to no constructive work due to appalling weather. On 11th May, with the thermometer reading -26°C, a steady 30-knot wind from the north-east, and visibility down to 50 yards, we crept into our little tent, seven foot by seven foot, and prepared to sit out another spell of bad weather. A depot of food, fuel and other stores awaited us somewhere nearby, if we could but find it, and dreaming as usual of warm fires and hot stews, we fell asleep.

We had no idea then that over two weeks later we would still be sitting in that tent – the coldest, the longest and the hungriest two weeks of my entire life. Our sleeping bags were forever damp from showers of hoar frost within the tent, the radio communication was abysmal, and we had pretty much exhausted our repertoire of conversation topics during the earlier lie-ups. The highlight of our waking hours would be venturing out to feed the dogs, but this excitement was tempered day by day as we witnessed them growing thinner and more lethargic. Our own

hunger was difficult enough to cope with, but theirs was heartbreaking. As we ran out of Nutty bars to feed them, we even began sharing some of our own paltry rations with them – a crazy thing to do under the circumstances, but then, without the dogs we were alone and stranded. Our moods fluctuated between acute boredom and acute fear.

At last visibility cleared a little and in desperation we headed out on a compass bearing, using anything to hand – ski poles, shovels, etc. – to mark our route. We eventually spotted the depot – not more than a mile away. One of the dogs, "Ena", could barely move by this time, and as we lifted her onto the sledge she felt light as a feather. We eventually made it to the depot, salvaged the supplies and recamped just before the weather closed in again. During the next few hours we gave the dogs several feeds, but Ena was badly weakened and, over the radio, Stonington vet Bob Bostelmann advised us to give her only sugar and water. Tragically we were too late and Ena died a short while later.'

*Dave Burkitt, Stonington, 1973*

A training run with the Orange Bastards on the pressure ice off Stonington Island.
'The dogs love this sort of travel as long as the loads are not too heavy. For them it is interesting, with lots of route finding to do. "Rover", the lead dog, has a tight trace to get away from "Bouncer" and "Sister" and the rest of the team are hidden behind the rafted up lump of sea ice. The route to the Plateau is seen as a narrow strip of snow just above Sister's tail.'

*Kevin Walton, Stonington, 1945/48*

'We had struggled through the so-called "Hinge Zone" of the Brunt Ice Shelf for two days trying to force a route known as the Wright Line, named after the man who had pioneered it. Jack Donaldson and Tony Stoneham were leading with the Hobbits team; myself and Ian Campbell were following with the Beatles. The plan was to find a safe route for tractors onto the inland ice, and we were marking each large crevasse with black flags. Within about three miles, however, we had run out of flags – the whole place was riddled, and we were forced to continue without markers.

At last we reached the steep exit slope of the Hinge and the worst appeared to be behind us. I shuffled alongside the sledge, and, glancing up, saw Jack gesticulating wildly in the distance, whilst Tony appeared to be sitting on the snow. My first assumption was that the Hobbits had somehow run off, but this idea was soon scotched as I drew closer and saw a crevasse, into which the dogs had fallen. The crevasse, five feet wide, had come in at right angles to our route, turned 90°, run parallel for about 50 yards and then turned at right angles again. The line was totally invisible and the team must have hit it exactly parallel. The heavy sledge had crashed through the bridge, pulling the team in after it. Jack told me that as the sledge had dropped from beneath him, his dongler rope had flipped off the handlebars, leaving him standing there.

I anchored my dogs and proceeded to set up a fixed rope, down which I could abseil to see if they were trapped on a bridge, but it was a forlorn hope. After about 20 minutes' descent the crevasse bellied out and once my eyes had become adjusted to the light, all I could see was a bottomless hole with the end of my rope swinging in space. There was no sound or movement from the depths: death must have been instant.

Some weeks later we managed to get tractors up to the site and rig up a winch system. We found the dead team 180 feet down. It had been a clear fall and that, plus the crushing weight of the sledge had done the damage. With a calmer mind I took a detailed look round the site. There was no indication of a crevasse line, nor evidence from flank marks; the zigzagging nature of the hole had proved lethal. The Hobbits were just desperately unlucky.'

*Dave Fletcher, Halley, 1978*

Finding a way through the 'Hinge Zone'.

*(Photo: Colin Wornham, Halley, 1966/67)*

'There is no doubt in my mind that huskies are considerably more intelligent than people give them credit for. Probably much of this intelligence is linked to their ancestor, the wolf, and their instinct for survival. This intelligence was well demonstrated one day during a journey from Rothera to a refuge hut at Blaiklock Island – some 30 odd miles. Towards the end of the day I became increasingly exasperated with my lead dog "Sue". We were about five miles from Blaiklock, it was starting to get dark and she seemed determined to take us off course. I had never been to Blaiklock before but my map showed the position of the refuge clearly. If my reading was correct, Sue's course would bring us at least two miles further along the coast. Eventually I gave way to Sue's insistence as we were making no progress at all and I was becoming exhausted trying to enforce my will. From that moment on we headed in a straight line – and shortly found ourselves at the refuge. Sue, I discovered, had visited the refuge three years earlier as a pup. Even more remarkable, the sea ice conditions had been completely different and the route must have been difficult to recognise. On future journeys I learnt to trust her memory more and more.'

*Rick Atkinson, Adelaide and Rothera, 1975/78*

Heim Glacier between Blaiklock Island and Detaille Island.
'A typical moment in a day's travel. This is hard going. The lead sledge has been lightened to ease the trail breaking and a man has gone ahead to encourage the team who are having a struggle in snow up to their bellies. Seen here are the Vikings and the Ladies.'

*Ian Sykes, Stonington, 1967/68*

Sea ice presents a completely different set of hazards, and many a team of dogs and men has come to grief upon it. The freeze up happens in a number of different ways. If a cold 'snap' coincides with utter calm, the sea may freeze smooth and solid; if, on the other hand, the cold snap is followed by a heavy snowfall, the insulating layer slows the thickening of the ice – it looks firm but will break away very easily in an offshore gale. If it has frozen hard and has then been broken up by wind and current, the ice floes pile on top of one another to form ridges of rough ice that are difficult to cross. The general rule at any island base is to wait until the ice has survived a gale before making any passages offshore. Only a handful of men have undergone the – usually accidental – initiation to the 'Antarctic Swimming Club', and dogs, too, though considerably more resistant to cold than men, preferred to stay on dry land.

The Spartans during a local sealing trip on the sea ice near Stonington.
'This scene is typical of Marguerite Bay in early spring. The old ice, although still many feet thick, begins to break up and to move, due to wind, tide and movement of the glacier foot. Pressure ridges rise up in fantastic shapes and provide interesting sledging which the dogs love. Cracks open and refreeze with black ice, and areas of melt water collect on top. This provides an assault course for gymnastic sledging but without the arch dangers of the crevasse. In this case, with all the dogs on the other side, it was necessary to nose the sledge to the ice edge and get the dogs to jerk it across.'

*Peter Forster, Stonington, 1957/61*

'In 1971 two weeks after midwinter's day Malcolm McArthur and I, with the Picts and Spartans teams, were making our way back from Marguerite Bay across the sea ice to Stonington. We had camped 20 miles from base on Reluctant Island, glad to have solid gravel under our feet, close to the larger, steep-sided Horseshoe Island. It had been a still and bitterly cold night, with a full moon. Our isolation was complete, but we had no sense of loneliness. Sledging with dogs, whatever other emotions you may experience – and they range from love and admiration to fury and despair – you are never lonely.

When we broke camp in the early hours of the morning, the brilliant glow of the Tilley lamp caused the blackness to close in like a threatening crowd. The dogs were shadowy forms, stretching and shaking the snow out of their coats, and beyond them was outer darkness. By the time I gave the command "Up dogs, huit!" smoky pinks and yellows were creeping up the sky behind the tumbling peaks of Pourquoi Pas Island. The surface of the sea ice was good and the dogs pulled with enthusiasm, perhaps sensing that we were homeward bound.

The first setback occurred when we reached a patch of newly frozen ice, smooth as a pane of glass and without wrinkle or blemish. It was impossible to stop the skis and sledge and the dogs could gain no purchase whatsoever. When they tried to pull, their four legs shot from under them and they sprawled bewildered on their bellies. Before long, mutiny was in the air and when finally I gave the order to swing back onto the old ice, my team turned as one. There was nothing for it but to follow the old ice towards the coast and hope that conditions might improve.

Sure enough, before long we came to a surface of solidly frozen ice floes, on which we could once more travel seaward. Not far ahead was the rocky headland of Camp Point, where there was an old food depot we had been asked to check. However, as I rounded the headland, looking for a suitable place to go ashore, I felt a floe sink beneath me. Before I could react, a raft of ice had tilted beneath my feet and I found myself immersed in icy water. Close to land, pressure from the sea beneath had become too much for the gigantic crazy

When the snow-covering melts over sea ice, it forms fresh water pools which often refreeze in turn to form a hard, smooth and slippery surface. In this picture, these conditions can be seen to have completely fazed poor 'Athos', leader of the Spartans. *(Photo: Ian McMorrin, Stonington, 1962/64)*

paving on which we were travelling. The floes had been forced apart and the "cement" had reverted to a semi-frozen skin in which they floated. The only hope was to keep the sledge moving, but now the dogs began to fall between the floes. As they panicked and ceased to pull, the sledge lost way until eventually it too slid sideways off a floe and began to settle into the thin skin that was covering the sea.
The situation seemed critical. Expecting the sledge to sink at any minute, I quickly cut the main trace and unclipped the dogs from their side traces, lest they drown. To my surprise, however, the sledge, though well and truly embedded, did not sink completely. Hope dawning, I attached a rope to it and, crawling from floe to floe, made my way towards the shore 30 yards away. After several fresh duckings, I discovered that I was safe enough on the larger floes so long as I did not try to stand up; landing proved awkward since the last floe, heaving on a slight swell, was separated from the sloping bank of smooth slippery ice by three feet of water. The floe was small and the bank steep, so if I fell in I should be unable to climb out again. Taking no chances, I leant cautiously over the gap and cut hand and foot holds with an ice axe before delicately transferring myself to the shore. In front was a ten foot wall of vertical ice which demanded more step cutting. Then, teeth chattering and toes numb, I set out to look for Malcolm.

Seeing my plight in time, he had returned to the far side of the headland. Now I found him in a position little better than my own, 40 yards out, among loose floes, with the rear of his sledge half under water. Fortunately, his dogs had not broken through as well and before long our combined efforts had heaved the sledge safely onto dry land. My feet needed immediate attention, but they soon came back to life in the warmth of Malc's sleeping bag and, without wasting any more time, we scrambled back over the broken rocks of the point.

I had been fearing the worst but the sledge was just as I had left it, and the Picts, for once too frightened to fight, had remained huddled anxiously together on a large floe; all that is except "Chinook", a large, cheerful, but relatively timid dog, who appeared to have been sent to Coventry as he sat in

splendid isolation on a small floe of his own. The first task was to clip the dogs back onto the main trace – not easy in the confined space of an ice floe, with eight dogs trying to lick me to express their pleasure at my return.

That done, I fastened a rope to "Morag" at the front of the trace and, with Malcolm pulling on the other end, they ran ashore with surprisingly little difficulty, hauling each other out of the water as they fell in. Next, each dog had to be heaved up the ice wall and dropped down the far side. It was quite some time before the team was finally spanned in the steep-walled gully beyond. That left the sledge to be rescued. I unloaded it, on hands and knees, while Malcolm hauled tent, boxes and sledge-bags ashore with the rope. At last, with the aid of a pulley system, the lightened sledge could be tipped onto a floe and righted.

By the time we could think of pitching the tent it had long been dark and the temperature was well down in the -20°Cs. Shaking from cold and exposure, I wriggled thankfully into my sleeping bag, only to experience excruciating pain as the frozen tissue of fingers, toes and knees thawed out. I slept very little that night.

I was badly frost-bitten but we decided to press on the following night in case the weather broke. We reached base just 24 hours after we had started at 5.30 in the morning. By midday the sky was overcast, and plumes of snow were blowing off the edge of the Plateau. The blow lasted eight days and when it ceased all the sea ice between Stonington and Camp Point had disappeared.'

*Rob Collister, Stonington, 1971/73*

Typical of sea ice conditions south of Hope Bay where a perfectly good snow surface is underlaid by snow sodden with sea water. If you stop, you sink – which can be seen to have happened here.

*(Photo: Geoff Renner, Stonington, 1964)*

Returning from a sealing trip across rotting sea-ice is not as risky as it looks. Away from the shore the pools between the floors are not deep. The dogs will happily jump the gaps, while the driver holds on and prays that the dogs don't stop. This is a picture of Ted Bingham and Alfred Stephenson, taken in 1937. Three days later the ice broke up and their ship came through.

*(Photo: W E Hampton, BGLE)*

Not everyone was lucky when it came to the perils of sea ice . . .

'On the 28th May 1958, Henry Wyatt and I were returning to Stonington from a six-week survey journey when a base radio call informed us that all contact had been lost with a three-man party somewhere between Horseshoe Island and the Dion Islands. Stan Black, Dave Statham and Geoff Stride had left the previous day on seemingly firm sea ice; but a strong wind had blown up suddenly and had cleared to reveal a ghastly expanse of open black water. Deeply shocked, we headed quickly back to Stonington where we could maintain radio watch and be available to form a search party.

On the night of 6th June we heard that "Yana", a bitch pup from one of the missing teams, had returned to Horseshoe. She was exhausted, and still in harness. Every man wished that husky could talk; but, alas, she could tell us nothing. Base leader John Paisley and the other men at Horseshoe spent hours searching for her tracks with lanterns, but it was not until morning that they could follow them out into Lystad Bay where they disappeared.

Search parties were being mobilised all round the area, including one of our own, but a treacherous gale blew up, with open water reported from Bongrain Point south to Contact Peak and Lagotellerie Island. Little progress was made. Then, two more dogs were sighted at the Argentine station on the Debenham Islands, 20 miles to the south-east, and hearts again surged with hope. Henry and myself with the Admirals team, and Nigel and Keith with the Churchmen, immediately headed up north to check the area. We didn't find them but on the coast of Millerand we did find bitch "Cloe": the Argentines based there reported that she had arrived six days previously, iced up and very hungry – this would have been the same day that Yana came into Horseshoe. The Argentines had their own party who were lucky to have returned safely from the Terra Firma islands, for the ice was rapidly breaking up behind them. A few days later, on the 17th, the dogs spotted by the Argentines came into Stonington and were recognised as "Ruth" and "Angus". Both were wearing harness, but Angus' trace had been cut or bitten while Ruth's harness was complete with trace and attaching ring. It was possible that the ring twisted clear of the cliphook, but more likely that she had been released. If so, it followed that the traces of harnesses on the other dogs had probably been cut by men, not sheared by dogs' teeth.

On the 20th, on some small islets in Square Bay, we found two more dogs: "Cocoa" and "Umiak". They were thin; Umiak with no harness, Cocoa with trace chewed six inches from his collar and harness still on but chewed over the back. Wagging tails and whines communicated their joy to see us but no details. We completed searches of all landings south of Horseshoe and returned to that base on the 25th to make plans with John Paisley for a search up to the Dion and Faure Islands as soon as the new ice permitted. Three days later, "Bessie" and "Cockie", both from Dave Statham's team, came in. Though we didn't know it then, they were the last surviving members of the party. Neither dog wore a harness, but both were in good condition, Cockie with blood on his coat, indicating that they had probably been living off penguins. Frank and I went out to look for their trail but the surfaces were too hard to make out tracks. We continued to search for many more days but conditions were treacherous, and changing all the time. Eventually we were forced to abandon hope.

Only those ten dogs knew what really happened out there. We must surmise from the evidence. In my view the party never reached Cape Bongrain on the night of 27th May as they had planned. The storm caught them before they could make a beach landing. Almost certainly the men had cut the dogs' traces during the break-up so that each could fight for himself – it was an unselfish act that saved most of the dogs' lives, but nevertheless a tragedy that none of us will forget.'

*Peter Gibbs, Stonington, 1956/58*

'It was a clear, fiercely cold day at the end of winter. After months of blizzards and darkness, we could at last set out on an expedition, and the chance to stand in the bright sun, to witness our departure, had been seized by all stationed at the base. Everyone stood tense and shivering, their breath hanging like ghosts before their faces in the still air. The diesels of the three brilliant red Muskegs were throbbing out on the snow to the south of the base. Behind them lay the great Maudheim sledges, neatly stacked with fuel drums, food boxes, equipment cases. Closer to the base were three dog teams lined up side by side: the Mobsters, the Beatles and the Hairybreeks, tiny by comparison with the machines, but somehow more comforting, more personal. The frantic excitement of being harnessed up had died away and the dogs were already bored by the interminable comings and goings. They lay in groups, occasionally yawning, sometimes growling or shuffling around in the snow to find an easier position, their eyes bright, watchful, ready.

Despite the apparent calm, Geoff Lovegrove and Tony Haines were standing nervously over the Mobsters, an argumentative team who fought every time they were harnessed to a sledge. "Nanuck", their old leader, stood alone at the head of the team, his bones twisted with rheumatism, despite the combination of care and penicillin. Though he now allowed his head to dip almost to the snow, he was still a leader: his knowledge and experience outclassed all the other dogs in the team. As an insurance policy, Geoff had been spending hours in the narrow, vicious days of winter working with one of the younger dogs to teach him the skills of leadership – but there was a long way to go. This morning the team seemed less boisterous, awed by the occasion or perhaps sympathetic to the old leader's mood.

Lew Jukes, his thin body wrapped in extra layers of clothing, was fondling "Bodach", leader of the Hairybreeks, who, at the order "Monte whore", rolled over on his back and waved his legs in the air. Doc John Wilson, stood at the back of the sledge in brand new windproofs, his arms gripped around himself, his back hunched against the cold – Doc never stopped looking cold. Dai Wild, an old hand at exploring, and I, his novice, were standing around nonchalantly waiting for the off; Dai in darned and dirty windproofs – he was saving the good stuff for mountain rescue in North Wales when he returned – and me in my shiny new ones. Dai could drive his team, the Beatles, around the base with great precision, turning them on sixpence, stopping and starting them when he wished, leaving them on their own for minutes at a time.

Eventually we were ready. Brian "Shreddy" Porter, leader of the tractor team, leaned past Jeremy Bailey, bent over his ice depth radar, exchanged signals to Dai and the other drivers and pushed his Muskeg into gear. With a jolt, a roar and great puffs of exhaust the three Muskegs moved forwards, each followed by three laden Maudheims, at a magnificent two miles an hour. They were followed by the Mobsters and the Hairybreeks. Then it was our turn. "Let's give them a good start," said Dai to me under his breath. It was necessary to whisper – "Suaq", leader of the Beatles, had long since

Breaking up a dog fight.

(Photo: Rod Rhys Jones, Halley, 1965/66)

recognised the words commonly used at the start of a day's sledging. Even the click of ski-bindings would start the dogs racing headlong across the snow.

When the tractors and the other teams were about 300 yards ahead, Dai shouted, "OK, boys." The dogs charged forward, almost falling over themselves. The acceleration was fantastic; the rush of snow under the runners; the thud of paws crushing crystals of ice; pure sweet, cold air pouring into the lungs. The dogs, tails in the air, shoulders bent forwards, tongues hanging from side to side, yelled with glee like children.

But as we relaxed into the excitement, the dogs suddenly stopped, as if ordered by some secret signal, and erupted into a vortex of snapping, squealing and snarling; all white teeth and eyes, flickering tongues and clawing feet. Only "Snowy" kept clear: she ran around the outside of the mêlée, mixing up all the traces and taking sly little nips at the buttocks of the fighting dogs. Dai and I grabbed equalisers – two-foot lengths of half-inch hemp rope doubled and bound – and waded into the fray. If the dogs are not stopped quickly they tear at the vulnerable groin, the ears and paws. They may not kill each other, quite, but they can stop a dog working for weeks. No quarter is given and none expected.

We were both enveloped in a writhing sea of dogs. Blood spattered onto the snow as their sharp teeth began to grip. One dog deep under the pile, attacked from all sides, gave up and began screaming with fear. Dai and I larruped and shouted to no avail. I tore off my mittens so that I could use my hands to unclip each dog from the trace, wrenching him from the fight and throwing him bodily out of the tumbling pile. I dived in to grab another dog. A jaw crushed the knuckles of my right hand. I hit the dog's nose hard and he let go. I was mad and I let them know it. Within a few minutes the severely chastened dogs were lying down licking the blood from their paws – as if butter wouldn't melt in their mouths.

A few hours later, we were up and on our way again; but that fight was to prove a bad omen. Nanuck died sometime on the second day out. He had been unable to lead after the first hour but had run along beside the sledge. With each passing hour he fell further and further behind. The first night he reached the tents several hours after we had set up camp. The second night he did not appear. Despite resting up for two further days in a spring blizzard we never saw him again.

Footnote: Dai Wild never got to use his new windproofs. He, John Wilson and Jeremy Bailey were all killed later in the expedition when the tractor they were driving fell through a snow bridge into a crevasse.'

*Rod Rhys Jones, Halley, 1965/66*

Four of eight teams that left Stonington for a five-month summer field trip in 1971.

*(Photo: Rob Collister, Stonington, 1971/73)*

'Time and estimated distance now told me that we should be near Jenny Island, though the darkness and fog was of no help. I did not relish over-shooting the island on its western side and onwards into a frozen ocean. Earlier, and on more than one occasion, my lead dog "Signy" had broken away from the preferred course I had set; I was aware too, that she was unsettled. "If she breaks away again," I thought, "I'll let her go." It was not long before she turned once more eastwards and only minutes later I began to hear the faint howl of distant huskies greeting each other out of a polar night – a sound that enraptures all who have experienced the polar wastes in the company of husky dogs. Earlier, the dogs' acute sense of smell had already told them we were home.'

*John Noble, Stonington, 1966/67*

The Spartans on the Churchill Peninsula, Graham Land east coast. This photograph was taken shortly after midnight on Christmas Eve, with the sun in the south, well above the horizon.

*(Photo: Ian McMorrin, Stonington, 1962/64)*

'Two men, 20 dogs, two dog sledges and one Nansen man-haul sledge – a starting load of 1,700 lb becoming 2,300 lb when we picked up 600 lb at the top of the hill three miles away. The power pack consisted of two dog teams, 11 in my team and nine in Frank Preston's. Our task was to take the load and lay a depot north of Adelaide Island base.

There could not be a greater difference in dog teams than between the Counties driven by Frank and my team the Giants. The Counties were old, powerful, reliable and well trained. Eight of the Giants on the other hand were barely a year old and had only 200 miles sledging to their credit. When asked how I drove such a young team my standard answer was "Approximately!"

The sky that morning was overcast and we only had the gloomy light of an August winter's day to help us load the sledges. The wind was slight but blowing from the north, and our course would eventually be upwind. The weather looked unpromising but we decided to harness up and travel as far as we could. As we ground up the first steep slope out of base we passed the other dogs on the spans and I avoided the hurt reproachful looks that were thrown at me by 20 miserable huskies temporarily confined to barracks.

At the top of the steep section of the slope I stopped to pick up my extra load and hitch on a trailer sledge with three empty oil drums lashed to it. These were destined to be survey beacons and their bulk forced me to use another sledge. Turning round I saw Frank had picked up his share of extra boxes and we both now had our complete loads.

The route from Adelaide leads east, following a crevasse-free slope about a mile wide up on to the relatively flat Fuchs-Ice Piedmont. On each side of the slope the ground falls away rather more quickly to finish in an ice cliff, averaging well over 100 feet high. In addition, all the ground within half a mile of the cliffs is riddled with crevasses.

Bearing almost due east across the wind was no problem and we moved steadily along. The ground drift increased slightly as we climbed and occasionally the dogs would almost disappear into a swirling blanket. We covered two miles and I then stopped for a breather and turned round to find "Lance", Frank's lead dog, just alongside me, using my sledge as a shelter from the wind.

I decided to try the dogs into the wind for a bit, and with an "Irra! Irra! Annie", we started off. Annie, my lead dog, turned gamely into the drift. After 100 yards or so, however, the first three dogs behind her started to balk and edge off the eye of the wind. Despite repeated commands, they gradually wove round to the east again. After that things happened very quickly: they continued their swing till facing almost south – then took off down the slope and down wind.

I passed Frank going in the opposite direction. At that time I could still raise a flicker of amusement at the surprised expression on his face; but any humour in the situation disappeared when I found my foot brake was no use and my repeated "Aaahh nows" were equally ineffectual.

The team was now out of control and my only recourse was to try to overturn the sledge. Unfortunately I had loaded up with dog food, which is very heavy and compact, giving a low centre of gravity with good stability. I only succeeded in exhausting myself. During one attempt, a painful bang on my ankle reminded me of the trailer sledge, which was now behaving like a mad thing, bucking on sastrugi and swinging wide to overtake me at intervals on each side. The sledge moved quicker as the slope steepened, almost bouncing over hard frozen waves of snow. It required all my energy to stay aboard.

I knew that the course I was on led to severe crevassing and a sheer cliff. I seemed to have only one option – to stop braking, let the sledge overrun the dogs and allow the trace to stop it. This would probably have worked at the expense of damaging some dogs but as, at that moment, they were all hell bent for destruction, tails up and thoroughly enjoying themselves, I had no choice.

Just as I stopped braking, the sledge gave a buck and a twist. I swung sideways to help it on its way and the next thing I knew I was hanging by my elbows on the insubstantial cornice which was all that remained of a crevasse bridge. About six yards further down the slope the sledges lay on their sides surrounded by a fantastic gaggle of dogs.

How to get out of here? Try pulling up gently on the cornice? No good – kangaroo pouch is too full of useless necessities. Kick out with my feet backwards and try to bridge the crack with my body? No good. Try again. Ah! A purchase for one foot, then the other, and I was bridged across the crack in a reasonably comfortable position, with time to think and a disturbing view right down a deep crevasse. Before I could assess my position properly I heard Frank shout and, looking to my right, just caught a glimpse of him in the gloom as he thundered down the slope out of control. It was reassuring to hear him shout, "Hang on!" but I reckoned he had troubles of his own and eventually I managed to slide gently out of the hole by traversing to the right and pulling up where the bridge was still complete and more solid. As I crawled down to the sledge I met Frank prodding his way up the slope and after a few seconds of mutual "I thought you had had it!"s we roped up and returned downhill to Frank's sledge.

Frank had experienced a similar incident. His sledge had also overturned as it broke through a crevasse. Fortunately it was a narrow one and his sledge was lying across it. One of his dogs had broken through and fallen out of his harness. Poor old "Nebro" was sitting on a bridge 15 feet below, looking up at us with a most mournful expression on his face. Frank looked after the rope on top and I climbed down to be greeted and licked with great glee by Nebro. After much hauling, heaving and pushing we eventually retrieved Nebro. We sorted Frank's sledge and dogs out so that they faced uphill again. Frank drove his team up to mine and we spent the next half hour sorting my sledge out.

During all this time the wind and drift had been increasing. This deterioration in the weather dictated a course set back to base. Nebro had not finished making trouble, however, and now escaped from his harness and ran off. No amount of enticement would attract him back; and, as we watched him circling the sledge, he suddenly plopped out of sight about 200 yards away.

All the business of re-picketing the sledges and roping together had to be carried out all over again. We were quite certain Nebro had fallen down a crevasse and so, with Frank leading, we prodded our way through the drift to where he had disappeared. Just as I thought Frank had reached the spot, I saw him leap backwards, turn round and wave me back to the sledge. As he explained later, "The snow suddenly ended and space began!" Nebro had added a fall over a 100-foot ice cliff to his already eventful day.

We now had to return to base and within the hour that's where we were welcomed by Nebro who had walked back to base on the sea ice. He had chosen his own way. There was not a mark on him and he had certainly taken the fastest and easiest way home.

That night Nebro sat in front of the stove while a whisky bottle passed not infrequently over his head. After three days in the hut for observation he was returned to the dog lines and the next week left on the depot run replay.'

*Gordon McCallum, Adelaide, 1962/63*

The Vikings descending the North-East Glacier at full tilt.

*(Photo: Ian Sykes, Stonington, 1967/69)*

One or two dogs undertook much longer solo excursions . . .

'At the end of 1958 the base at Detaille Island was closed. Even with the assistance of two American icebreakers *Biscoe* could not reach the station. So having secured it against the elements, Brian Foote's party sledged their belongings out over 30 miles of sea ice to the ship. As the dogs were being hoisted on board, "Steve" escaped and refused to be caught. Instead he set off for home along their sledge tracks, thus sealing his fate for there was no time to organise a round-up. It was a very sad ending, and the drivers who had loved and worked with him felt it keenly.

Nearly three months later everyone at Horseshoe was astounded to see Steve running happily over the hill, fit and well, and delighted to be the centre of such an enthusiastic welcome. From his good condition it was clear that he had returned to

Detaille and lived on the old seal pile from which the dogs had been fed. As midwinter approached and still his friends failed to return, he must have decided to go and look for them. He could have gone west to the ice edge or he might have turned north or east. Instead he surely remembered making the 60-mile sledge journey to Horseshoe the previous season and confidently set off south. Since no vestige of a trail could have remained, he had to remember the intricate route, across the sea ice of Lallemand Fjord, over the glaciers of the Arrowsmith Peninsula, down into Bourgeois Fjord, and so to Horseshoe Island and the base lying in a bay on the west coast. In winter there was no food along the route, and it is astonishing that a dog should take a conscious decision to seek company and abandon his larder on the strength of a past memory. So much for those who believe dogs cannot think.'

*Extract from* Of Ice and Men *by Sir Vivian Fuchs*

A camp on the Byway Glacier, 1956.

'This was a steep glacier which curved round a mountainous bluff so that the crevasses were numerous and large. The glacier descended into Darbel Bay, right on the Antarctic Circle on the west coast of the Antarctic Peninsula, and not far from Detaille Island. The surveying of Darbel Bay, with its ring of formidable peaks and glaciers, had been delayed for many years because only three out of the 20-odd jumbled glaciers looked like being even remotely negotiable, and the ice on the bay itself was highly unreliable. On this occasion, John Thorne and I managed to make a jolting descent from the spine of the Peninsula down what is now called Erskine Glacier, and met up with Denis Goldsmith and Ossie Connochie on one of the islands in the bay where they had been cut off by open water. Then all four of us, with the two dog teams, found a route by Byway Glacier to the Plateau again, sledged south along it, and eventually returned to Detaille, keeping a running survey going on the way. Throughout this hazardous journey, the dogs were sure-footed and steady, whether on glacier or sea-ice, and my lead dog, "Bodger", led the whole way, obeying my steering orders with an accuracy which surprised even me.'

*Angus Erskine, Detaille, 1956/58*

# CHAPTER TEN
# A ROUTINE TO LIVE BY

*'If you camp and travel efficiently you will spend about 80% of every 24 hours camping and travelling, leaving the rest for work. If you camp and travel inefficiently, you will spend 90% of every day camping and travelling — the result of this will be that the working time is halved.'*

Dr Charles Swithinbank

Routine is a dull word, but spend a year or two working in Antarctica, and you soon learn to swear by it. On a calm day, with blue skies and a well trained dog team out ahead, it was possible to reach a sense of working harmony that is rarely surpassed. However, the weather was fickle and could change all too rapidly. For this reason all field units had very similar systems for calling a halt to travel, pitching camp and making it blizzard-proof at a moment's notice. 'Rules' of what to do and how to do it were never written down; they evolved in the early years and that formula for success, equally applicable in good weather or bad, has changed little over the years.

For three reasons – sanity, sociability and safety (the greatest of these being safety) – a field unit always consisted of two men. Occasionally, for short journeys, they might use a single dog team, but invariably two teams and two sledges were necessary. Imagine the scene:

Two dog teams and two men in the middle of a featureless white plateau, travelling steadily on a good, hard surface. There is little noise – the panting of weary dogs, an occasional command issued, but that is all. At precisely 5 p.m., as agreed some hours before, the lead team stops. The weather is settled so those earlier plans have not had to be changed. The second sledge pulls up alongside the first one, several metres away from it. There's no time for a chin-wag: two teams side by side is asking for trouble, weary though the dogs may be. With little conversation, each man

stretches out and pickets the centre trace and the night spans, and each dog is clipped into its respective place. The order is the same every day in an attempt to place compatible dogs side by side and to keep bitches in season well out of harm's way! Some harnesses are then removed and hung in a bunch on the back of the sledge.

Once the dogs are safely tethered there is a chance to discuss the day just ended. This discussion will be short; these two men have been out from base for nearly two months so there is probably not much left to be said! The tent is taken off one sledge and erected – again there is no discussion about who is to do what: the same routine has been operating since the men left base.

It is now time to feed the dogs, and this is very much a joint venture. It is definitely *not* good psychology to feed one team without the others receiving their ration at the same time – a concerted effort by the dogs to rectify the situation could result in the jerking out of the snow stakes holding the spans. Eighteen weary and hungry animals aware that the box of Nutrican is being opened is a sight to behold – instantly they become alert, eagerly awaiting their share.

One of the two men has been allocated 'inside' duties, the other 'outside' duties, and these will be his for the duration of 24 hours, a switch-over effected at the end of the working day, or at 4 p.m. if blizzard bound. The inside man now dives into the tent – his objective is to create a cosy home environment and he has about 15 minutes to do it! First of all he lays out the groundsheet. Then, two 'P' (personal) bags are passed in, each one containing a lilo, sheepskin and sleeping bag. Five or so minutes later, a 'bed' is neatly laid out along each side of the tent. Without a word being spoken, the outside man will know when to pass in the first box containing primus stove, paraffin lamp, etc., so that the cooking area can be arranged, the stove lit and some snow melted for that all-important mug of tea. Next in goes the food box – containing enough food for several days without having to venture outside. Then goes the tent box with those precious diaries, books, etc. Finally, the radio box is passed in. As the water heats up, the ritual takes place of spreading rock-hard butter, perhaps slightly softened if it has been standing near the primus for a couple of minutes, onto 'sledging' biscuits. Marmite and dried onions are then spread sparingly on top. Six biscuits are prepared and very soon a cup of tea has been brewed to accompany them.

'The heaviest items – dog food, man food, radio, theodolite, paraffin, stove and cooking utensils – form the lower layer on the sledge to make it more stable and reduce the risk of a sledge overturn. The sledge is secured by passing a rope across the load and through the rope loops attached to each side of the bridges. The final knot is always tied on top of the load so that it can be easily undone in the event of an overturn.'

*Alan Wright, Adelaide, 1961/63*

Meanwhile, the outside man has been busy, too. He finishes erecting the tent, staking out all the guy ropes and hauling them taut. Spare ration boxes are placed on the valance to prevent the wind from lifting it. Snow blocks are cut and placed between the tent inner and outer, just to the right of the entrance, and well away from the two-gallon paraffin can just to the left of the door. The radio aerial that hangs out of the ventilator tube near the top of the pyramid is unwound and set up, keeping the end (or two ends if it is a dipole) well clear of the snow. All items not in use are lashed to the sledges. The two groups of dog harnesses are passed inside so that they can dry out overnight in the top of the tent. At last it is time to leave the great outdoors for the warmth of 'home'!

Once inside, the scene is familiar. Indeed the scene should be almost exactly the same whoever is on whichever duty. Out of courtesy, the inside man offers only unbroken biscuits to the outside man. Large mugs of steaming tea are consumed amid desultory conversation; layers of clothing are steadily peeled off and hung up to dry; preparation of the evening meal of dried meat bar stew begins. In general the scene is one of relaxation, warmth and relative comfort. The primus is perhaps allowed to go out for a while, leaving the Tilley lamp to heat and light the tent. But if that outside temperature falls much below -25°C, on comes the primus again.

And so the evening progresses. After supper: perhaps a radio sked with base, to advise them of the new camp position. Perhaps half an hour listening to the BBC World Service – the reception in Antarctica is wonderful. This might trigger a discussion of the news, or perhaps plans have to be discussed for the morrow. In the unlikely event that something needs attending to outside, no discussion is needed – it is the outside man who painstakingly dons his outer clothing, and disappears out through the sleeve entrance to sort it out. There are of course one or two exceptions . . .

The scenario described could be termed the ideal one. Many variations are possible. Perhaps plans have had to be changed in a hurry, with the travelling cut short as the weather deteriorated quickly and unexpectedly. Tethering out two dog teams and pitching a pyramid tent in -20°C degrees with 40 knots of wind and snow reducing visibility to ten metres is a hard task. When carried out by a team with a well tested and unvarying routine, these conditions may simply mean an unpleasant half hour. For an inexperienced team with no system, they may result in total tragedy – a tent blown away, dogs running amok. The possibilities are endless.

Making camp in ideal conditions.

*(Photo: Peter Forster, Stonington, 1957/61)*

Finding a suitable camp site is never easy. Unfortunately the scenic spots are not always the safest. Obvious places to avoid include the foot of potential avalanche slopes and ice falls, or on top of crevasse bridges or poor sea ice. Then there are other, more subtle considerations. For instance, a few feet one way or the other might mean the difference between staying clear of drifting snow and being completely buried.

The heyday of dog sledging.

'A number of sledge parties, having completed their summer field work, met up at the bottom of the Weyerhausen Glacier and prepared to return together the final 100 miles or so to Stonington. There are eight teams and approximately 75 dogs.'
*Ian Sykes, Stonington, 1967/69*

'The end of a good day – Dr Ian Gemmel and "Max" relax in the evening light on the Wright Peninsula. This was one of the last recreational runs before the dogs were removed.'

*Steve Cummins, Rothera, 1991/93*

'I had received permission from Dr Fuchs for a solo return trip to the glacier for weather observing. It was very uneventful, except for a blizzard. One night there was a lull in the blizzard and I looked out of the tent. The flying clouds had parted a little and the moon shone weakly, painting the glacier in a yellowish light. It seemed unreal: the strange mixture of light and shade, the dull gleam of the snow around, the darker shapes of mountains in the distance, and the glint of ice-fields here and there. A light breeze occasionally carried little willywas of drift along the glacier surface. Nothing but the tent breathed of civilisation. I withdrew into the tent and settled down to sleep. Then I felt something push the tent canvas in towards my feet. My heart missed a beat. What could it be? A species of the Himalayan Abominable Snowman that had emigrated to Antarctica? I propped myself up – yes, something was definitely pushing from the outside, and it wasn't the wind. My fingers shaking, I untied the sleeve entrance which formed a tunnel-like doorway, but before I could look outside, a huge snow-crusted and furry head was thrust inside, a long tongue launched itself out at me, and then a friendly "woof woof" – it was "Pretty". She had got away from base and backtracked up the glacier. I breathed a sigh of relief and pulled her inside with me. Eventually she left me, but later she came back and brought "Peter" with her, so I was not alone but had two rather pleasant visitors to whom I could talk without fear of being contradicted.'

*Ken Pawson, Admiralty Bay, 1947/49*

'Mimi' of the Giants team. Camped on the Fuchs-Ice Piedmont, Adelaide Island, 1961.

'In the height of summer, it is often easier to travel at night when the temperature drops and the surface freezes. The tent door is usually kept open while we sleep because it gets very stuffy, and on this occasion I was awoken very suddenly by Mimi jumping on top of me and proceeding to give my face a wash with her large tongue. My arms were trapped inside my sleeping bag, and I was held down by nearly 100 lb of husky. Alan Wright woke up and tried to throw her out. She identified his actions as a game and in her excitement peed copiously over my sleeping bag. The more he tried to push her out the more excited she became and the more she peed. She then decided to sprint in a circle round a six-foot square tent. Pots, pans, radio and primus were all sent flying. In desperation we both dived out of the tent and left her in command.'

*Gordon McCallum, Adelaide, 1962/63*

*(Photo: Roger Daynes)*

'Every now and then it was necessary to check the dogs didn't become snowed under; but sometimes we cheated: instead of togging up to go outside we sat up in our sleeping bags and imitated their wolf song; our heads back howling and crooning. The dogs could not help but reply; and soon the tent would be reverberating to the sound of their song. We knew that when they sang they sat or stood up, and that way cleared the snow off their heads . . . Going outside in the middle of the night was avoided at all costs. In blizzard conditions, when nature called, we removed the ground sheet in the tent and dug a hole in the snow, then stuck the spade in the ground with the shaft and handle at a perfect angle to support ourselves in a crouching position. Sometimes we defecated onto the other spade and, when the weather had cleared a bit, took it outside for the dogs – useful extra calories. It sounds disgusting, but in freezing temperatures turds lack the revolting properties they do in warmer climes.'

*Nick Cox, Rothera, 1979/81*

'Our travel rations were designed to be easily digestible, so that trips outside were minimal, and fast – "bare essentials" we called them. Nevertheless, those "essentials" could come under considerable attack, and not just from the weather. On one occasion we had been stuck in a tent in blizzard conditions for several days, and my tent partner Robbie Slessor's need to relieve himself increased until he was forced outside, his trousers half mast at the ready. Suddenly I heard the cry, "Roger! Roger! Go away, Roger!" Moments later Robbie crawled back into the tent. Roger, he informed me, had slipped his collar and was running loose; he had been "Very impatient – but very, very gentle."'

*Kevin Walton, Stonington, 1945/48*

'It was during one of my spells as "outside man" at the Mount Bransfield
Camp that I was most grateful for the presence of the dogs. It was my turn to
feed them and I had to venture out in an extremely strong blizzard. I should
have roped up, but this was my first sledging trip, and I suppose I didn't
appreciate the extent of the danger. Antarctica was about to teach me a
lesson I would not forget – after completing my rounds I was blown over and
lost all contact with the camp. I suppressed the urge to panic and
systematically tracked up wind, down wind and across wind, hoping to find a
trace of something I recognised. Nothing. Panic again threatened to engulf
me. Then I remembered the dogs' habit of singing in unison and with this in
mind I again tracked up wind to mimic their howling. As quickly as possible
in the prevailing conditions I tracked down wind and listened. After the
second attempt I was successful – the dogs answered my calls and told me
the direction of camp. My embarrassment at having been so careless as to get
lost in the first place meant that I did not tell my colleagues about my little
escapade; but from that moment I treated adverse weather conditions with
the utmost respect.'

*Alan Wright, Adelaide, 1961/63*

*(Photo: Ian McMorrin,*
*Stonington, 1962/64)*

'It was often the case that a calm "dingle" day deteriorated into a full blown blizzard within an hour. The most harrowing adventure of my sea ice travels with the dogs was heralded only by a few wispy lenticular clouds forming on distant peaks and a faint atmospheric halo round the sun. Very soon conditions were appalling and we were forced to make camp on the sea ice, knowing full well that camping away from land was to break the first rule of sea ice travel. We felt sure we were sufficiently far into Bourgeois Fjord to avoid immediate danger but with sea ice you can never be certain. Our radio communication with Adelaide Base that evening was almost impossible due to the incredible noise being generated by our pyramid tent as it took the full buffeting of the gale that was blasting down the fjord. What we could hear over the noise of the tent did nothing to bolster our confidence. Ric, the radio operator, reported somewhat anxiously that the sea ice had blown out from around Adelaide Island and that the wind was blowing at over 90 knots. The most alarming news came last. The temperature was +6°C! It wasn't unusual for the temperature to rise rapidly during a storm at this time of year but to rise from -30°C to +6°C in just six hours was rather extreme!

As the evening progressed the gale intensified. Although we were sitting only a foot apart, my sledging partner and I had to shout at each other if we wanted to be heard. But there was little to be said. It was like being inside a badly balanced spin dryer that was running full pelt. Gusts of wind continued to bombard the tent from all directions throughout the night.

Occasionally we would hear a whimper or cry from the dogs over the top of the howling gale. At one point rain lashed against the tent which then turned to hail and back to snow. There were times when we were sure we felt the ice moving and imagined ourselves floating out to sea. We were convinced that our tent was about to depart our company and we lay there with all our clothes on and our bags packed in anticipation of what seemed to be the inevitable.

As had many a pyramid tent before, our tent survived all that the Antarctic night could hurl at us. As the dawn broke the storm began to abate. The surroundings to our camp had been transformed over night. Where there had been snow there was nothing but ice. The wind had stripped the frozen surface of the sea. The dogs lay curled up tight on mounds of remaining snow. The sledges, still loaded with our emergency survival equipment, remained in place, firmly picketed to the ice. Fortunately for us the sea ice had held firm but not far to the west the ominous darkening of the horizon marked the presence of open water.

Long before the storm had petered out we had broken camp and our sledges were loaded. We had no intention of spending another night out on the ice. The dogs, true to form, had made light of the uncomfortable ordeal and their spirits were high. Once under way, they were soon limbered up and our progress across the icy surface as we headed for Blaiklock Island was a far cry from the pace of the previous day.'

*Rick Atkinson, Adelaide and Rothera, 1975/78*

Hoar frost covering sledge.

*(Photo: Roger Scott, Stonington, 1972/75)*

The morning after the night before. Digging sledge and equipment out of the snow often takes hours.

*(Photo: Ian Sykes, Stonington, 1967/69)*

'For ten days the blizzard raged. Enormous drifts piled up. Visibility was seldom more than ten yards and often less than two. Five dogs died during the third night. They had allowed themselves to be drifted over and had for a while a natural shelter, but the wind packed the snow like iron that night and the buried dogs had suffocated. One pair had died locked in a fight and were frozen so hard we could not tear them apart. We dragged them away, their stiff bodies scratching tracks in the snow, and heaved them by their tails to slide them the rest of the way on their own, to their grave – a breath gash in a smooth face of snow which opened and shut with the tides. '

*Extract from* A World Of Men *by Wally Herbert*

Five teams camped six miles from Stonington on Neny Fjord at the start of a 1,000-mile journey.

*(Photo: Ian McMorrin, Stonington, 1962/64)*

*[Overleaf]* Calm after the storm. Lenticular clouds over 'Trident' herald the end to a four-day lie up for Barry Wilson and the Admirals.  *(Photo: Charlie Siderfin, Rothera, 1992/94)*

# CHAPTER ELEVEN
# 'GROW-A-PUP'

*'Pups played noisily on the roof of the hut, stealing food,*
*chewing anything they found lying around and generally getting*
*in everyone's way. They were a major nuisance as well as being*
*the biggest boost to morale any Antarctic base could have.'*

Gordon McCallum, Adelaide, 1962/63

When base leader Vic Russell left Hope Bay in 1947, he was unknowingly turning a page in the history of Antarctic exploration: his departure was the first time that a team of fully trained huskies could be passed on to a successor and continue working in the field. On all previous expeditions, the dogs had had to be put down, or, in some special cases, had been brought back to civilisation as pets or as zoo exhibits. In his two years Vic Russell had watched the dog numbers increase from the original 25 brought down from Labrador, to well over 60. Similarly at Stonington Island, an initial 26 dogs had increased to nearly 80.

Very little thought was given to breeding policy in those early years. As field work expanded, so did the need for dogs. Breeding occurred in a haphazard fashion, with few formal records made, and new pups generally kept and introduced into the team as they came of age. In time it seemed sensible to encourage bitches to mate with the best dogs of their team, but if a dog slipped his collar when a party was in the field, it was a case of 'first come, first served'. Inevitably some in-breeding resulted, with pups mating with their mothers, but the process of natural selection more or less held good until a more organised breeding plan was adopted four years later.

Apart from one exchange of seven dogs, following the 700-mile journey from Hope Bay down to Stonington in 1947, the original dog stocks from Labrador had remained isolated. Following the fire at Hope Bay and the temporary abandoning of Stonington Base, all working dogs were redistributed. Some went for breeding to smaller offshore British bases such as the Argentine Islands, Admiralty Bay and Deception Island; some were shipped back to the UK to take part in the Festival of Britain's Dome of Discovery; and some, following quarantine in the UK, were handed on to the Norwegian British Swedish Antarctic Expedition. When Hope Bay was re-opened in 1952, 70 dogs were drawn back to form a nucleus, and an attempt was made to trace the genealogical tree of each. This proved extremely difficult, not least because sibling pups didn't necessarily have the same father; but from this point onwards all dogs were numbered, registered and allocated a card which recorded the date and place of birth, and mother and sire. This card was regularly up-dated with such details as the dog's team position, distances travelled, health and general performance, and a copy sent back to Britain at the end of each season.

'Gert' with her brothers and sisters in the puppy pit, Hope Bay, 1945. Gert was the first of 13 generations of Antarctic-born huskies. Her descendants were eventually flown to new homes in Canada in 1994.

*(Photo: Vic Russell, Hope Bay, 1945/46)*

Two young Vikings, 'Pinky' and 'Perky' at two months old.
*(Photo: John Noble, Stonington, 1966/67)*

Dog cards were a means of providing useful information to the changing base personnel and, more importantly, avoiding the dangers of in-breeding. By the end of the dog era in 1994, some 900 dog cards were held in the BAS archives and it was possible to trace the family tree back through 13 generations. In many ways they resembled school reports, and made entertaining reading.

| NAME: JOY | NO: D 3038/46 | DOG BITCH No registered number | FORN Jan '46 |
|---|---|---|---|
| Father CAPTAIN No — | Mother GERT No — | | Markings to be entered at age 12 months |

Medical History: This card was only started - 1952 when Joy was nearly six years old. All history up to 1952 is from Base dog reports.

Characters:

GOOD: A superb mother when it was finally possible to let her keep them. She was reprieved from 'culling' when Base E was closed to let her have pups. 1952 Very shy!
In her last year she graduated to team leader.

BAD: Frankly none. 1952

1955
Very arthritic not surprising after a long & active life.
Put down Apr 1955 — aged 9.

'A real "piss artist" who likes to turn round and examine his work once he has finished.'

Very much a one man dog —

Jumps off all four feet together when she gets excited.

He snores something terrible

Eats anything he can find, man made fibres appear just as appetising as natural ones. They all pass through unharmed.

130

## WORKING HISTORY: (position in team, major journeys, etc.)

( Gleaned from various base records)

First trained at 9 months Nov. 46 became second bitch in GANGSTERS.

| | |
|---|---|
| August – October 47 Depot laying for projected summer journey. | 400 miles |
| Oct 47 – Jan. 48. Hope bay to Stonington Island including much relaying. | 710 miles |
| March 48 remained with GANGSTERS at Stonington · Base E | |
| April 48 – August 48 semi local work | 310 miles |
| Sept 48 – Dec 48 King George VI Sound | 1100 miles |
| Jan 49 – Dec 49 Many local journeys plus summer and King George VI Sound | 1500 miles |
| Mch 50 Sent to Base H for breeding | |

Mch '52 Returned to Base D after 5 years with remains of the Gangsters and her two PUPS, ACE & SPUD.
Not used for Major journeys but as leader. 400 miles

Total miles 3420

### BASE TRANSFERS:

| Left Base | Date | Arrived Base | Date |
|---|---|---|---|
| D | Oct 47 | E | Jan 48 |
| E | Mch 50 | H | Mch 50 |
| H | Mch 52 | D | Mch 52 |

## PROGENY: (by litter, names and numbers. Give name and No. of other parent)

Sire COLONEL.  12 Pups during journey to Stonington. All destroyed. 13.11.47 (12)

Sire MUTT  5 Pups all destroyed born on the trail 13.10.49 (5)

Sire COLONEL (or possibly FLASH) 22.4.50.
two pups  ACE  H 3025/50
SPUD  H 3026/50 (6) 2

Sire ACE (or possibly SPUD)
(This was an
error. Sires
were her pups)
CHOPPER ♂ D 3011/52
MARIE ♀ D 3008/52
MILLIE ♀ D 3009/52

Sire YAP.  D 3034/50  22.4.53
SIS ♀ D 3017/53 (4)
SHEP ♂ D 3018/53  2

Total no. of pups— 34
Pups retained to adulthood – 7

Pups born in brackets retained not in brackets.

---

Very, very sensitive. If you talk to him firmly he will attempt to lick your hand to the bone by way of apologising.

A real escape artist who always returns to his own place and pretends he is still tethered.

'Works like ten, fights like ten.'

Jumps up at one by way of greeting with all four feet in the air and will knock you over.

Massive chap but gets very hungry

In 1954 the British North Greenland Expedition was ending and 15 of their dogs were shipped to Antarctica, together with three from Canada and three who had been born in England. To the casual observer there is probably little to choose between one sledge dog and the next: to a dog driver who has so many miles of difficult terrain to cover, the differences are important and a source of much debate. A comparison between these three groups therefore provided a stimulus for a theoretical consideration on what constituted the 'ideal husky with a view to establishing a proper breeding policy for the BAS dogs'.

Overall, the Antarctic-born dogs tended to be larger and with wider chests than those originally brought down from Labrador in 1945 and '46, almost certainly due to the regular and nourishing diet of seal meat; but there were arguments both for and against this 'natural' evolution. Large dogs have a larger surface to weight ratio and so need proportionately less food to maintain themselves, whereas small dogs are faster and had a reputation for being more manageable in a team. A heavy dog is more likely to fall down a crevasse and also more difficult to pull out. Losing one out of a seven 'large dog' team is more dangerous than one from a nine 'small dog' team; but with seven dogs, less food is needed. The argument can go on.

In 1954 Julian Taylor, a science graduate from Cambridge, was appointed to Hope Bay as 'dog physiologist' with the broad remit to study the use of huskies in Antarctica and make recommendations. Taylor developed an electrical device to measure just how much pull a dog team could develop when working. Strain gauges were incorporated into the towing rope, producing some astonishing results: a team of nine dogs could exert a pull of about 130 lb force for a full eight-hour day – equivalent to about $1\frac{3}{4}$ horse power per team, and $\frac{1}{7}$ horse power per dog. Taylor was also able to show that a dog's steady pull was not directly related to his weight; in fact in many cases a small 'solid' dog could out-pull a much

larger one. His estimate of an 'optimum' sledge dog for field work in the Antarctic was therefore as follows:

> Height at shoulder: 23" (58.5 cm)*
> Nose to tail: 60" (152.5 cm)
> Shoulder width: 10" (25.5 cm)
> Hip width: 8" (20.32 cm)
> Weight: approx. 90 lb

* All figures were around 10% lower for bitches.

These were the figures adopted as a breeding policy that by and large was maintained for the next 40 years. A list of potential sires – selected as much for intelligence as for size – would be kept updated and pinned to the base notice board at all times, and drivers were expected to stick to it. At base, a bitch would be penned with a potential mate for a few days; in the field, for the sake of a peaceful night, the couple would be tethered well away from the others. These and other guidelines formed the basis for a BAS manual amusingly entitled *Grow-a-Pup*.

In time, the smaller island bases were developed as breeding centres. Here, an abundance of seals provided the fresh meat so necessary for healthy bitches and growing puppies in their first year of life. As well as this, the base routine was less demanding, and as long as there was no dangerous sea ice on which pups could wander and become lost, they could be allowed to roam freely and develop. Small bases also provided a happy retirement home for the older dogs with many thousands of miles of sledge-pulling to their credit. They proved excellent sires to improve and maintain the stock of future dogs, and appeared to draw great pleasure from maintaining discipline among growing puppies without having to go through the demanding routine of maintaining their 'kingship' as part of working teams.

Bitch 'Juno' at Adelaide Island, 1962.
'On two occasions "Juno" was mated as part of the breeding programme. She was given a comfortable kennel, fed extra rations, vitamins and cod liver oil. Her coat became glossy, her eyes maternal and she expanded appropriately. She seemed to enjoy the extra attention and the viewpoint from the top of the kennel. Her second phantom pregnancy was however her last chance at the easy life. She was charged with "Fooling the dog man and destroying his credibility", found guilty as charged and sentenced to a three-month survey trip on a diet of dried Pemmican.'

*Gordon McCallum, Adelaide, 1962/63*

'From the age of nine months, bitches would come on heat every six months or so, though breeding was not encouraged until they were two years old. This is "Pujok" feeling very sorry for herself – huskies hate solitude and being away from the rest of the team.'

*Simon Gill, Rothera, 1986/92*

Roger Owen with two of six pups born to 'Bev'.
The gestation period for huskies is 63 days and mums were generally drawn out of the team at seven weeks. An average litter is between four and six pups, although the recôrd is 14 pups born to a bitch named 'Joy'. On very long journeys there were of course occasions when both mating and pupping took place in the field. Mums were happy to go back to work after a day or so's rest, but would usually be returned, with pups, to base at the earliest opportunity.

*(Photo: Roger Owen, Adelaide, 1964)*

'Towards the end of May 1946, four of us and two dog teams were returning to Hope Bay following a short field trip. With 17 miles to go, we erected the two tents at "Swamp Camp", so-called because of its notorious flooded sea ice. After supper we heard one of the dogs being unusually noisy so I donned clothing and sealskin boots and went out to see what was wrong. It turned out to be "Pretty" who was making the fuss. We had known before we started the journey that she was pregnant but we had not thought she was due to whelp for some time yet. I released her from the span thinking that if she was going to pup, she had better make herself as comfortable as possible. This had evidently occurred to her too, for by the time I had checked on the other dogs and walked the five yards back to the tent, I found her already curled up on my sleeping bag and looking extremely comfortable. I turned her out, much against her will, but she wasn't going to give up that easily and continued to mooch around trying to find a way in. All of a sudden we heard chewing and ripping noises and realised that she was trying to eat her way through both outer and inner entrances of the tent! I looked up to find her nose just coming through; a second later, she was all in, and again making herself comfortable at the foot of my sleeping bag. We knew that she had won so I squeezed myself into the top end of the bag and eventually went to sleep – she made a splendid foot warmer. During the night I heard infant squeals and saw by torchlight that the pups had started to arrive. By breakfast time there were five beautiful pups, all flourishing. Pretty shared my breakfast porridge, produced a sixth pup and then enjoyed some bacon – she had earned it. We broke camp and carefully transferred Pretty and her new family on to a prepared nest of pullovers on one of the sledges, to ride triumphantly back to base.

*Vic Russell, Hope Bay, 1945/46*

'At 8 p.m. I went out to check on the dogs and found "Whitey" had started pupping. What a way for the poor blighters to start life! Straightaway we built a shelter of ration boxes and bits of canvas and each of us surrendered a garment as padding. The next day we had to lay up all day in a white-out and used the time to think of names for the pups: "Dumbo" and "Blitz". The following day we moved at about 11 a.m. with Whitey in harness running with the team and the pups in a box on the sledge. There was a panic when Whitey got away and started off back to the old camp site thinking that we had left the pups behind. Jumbo whipped a pup out of the box and pinched it so that it squeaked. Luckily Whitey heard and she came back to us.'

*Extract from Jack Reid's diary, Argentine Islands, 1949*

Weighing in at one day old.
At birth pups weighed about 12 oz but doubled this within three days. Rickets was quite common in the early days so the pups would be fed extra vitamins and cod liver oil.

*(Photo: Roger Owen, Adelaide, 1964)*

'My first bath.'

(Photo: Ian Sykes,
Stonington, 1967/69)

'Naming as many as 30 puppies a year was a
difficult task and frequently became the cause of
fierce argument. This one was easy enough,
though! She was born unexpectedly in a
blizzard, and when we found her she was very
cold. We popped her into one of our mukluk
boots and hung it above the stove. "Mukluk"
grew up to be a splendid, though timid breeding
bitch.'

Kevin Walton, Stonington, 1945/47

'During the winter of 1968 my lead bitch "Jenny" suffered serious problems while giving birth. There was no vet on base that season and in typical "Fids" fashion the base doctor attempted a caesarean section and managed to save two of the pups: Jenny survived the operation but never fully recovered and died a day or so later. No other mother seemed to want the new pups "Spike" and "Eccles", so we came up with the idea of the "Omnitit". Plans were high at the time that this wonderful invention would be the start of a thriving export business but strangely there were only a few takers. When they were old enough, the pups joined the Vikings team – they were the only fully man-reared dogs we found on the records.'

*Ian Sykes, Stonington, 1967/69*

The winter months were the preferred time of year for arrival of the pups – there was less opportunity for travel and more time to give them the attention they needed. It was important for pups to enjoy human contact, as this increased the chance of their becoming well adjusted, easy to manage dogs in adult life.

*(Photo: Rob Collister, Stonington, 1971/73)*

'Pups, as many as a dozen at a time, would sometimes be brought into the base hut whereupon they would immediately take control. House training was not in their vocabulary and chair legs and other suitable items were the objects of much attention. This would usually last for about half an hour before they crashed out fast asleep, and then started on the next round of fun.'

*Roger Scott, Stonington, 1972/75*

'Occasionally BAS dogs would be transferred to other bases. On this occasion Scott Base, New Zealand, requested two young animals for breeding purposes and they were sent "Stuart" and "Anthe" (whose name makes sense when combined with the other litter siblings, "Lady", "Anthe", "Tramp") from Halley Bay. Anthe produced pups 63 days after arrival – it is rumoured that her litter was conceived in the aircraft as it crossed the Pole!'

*Chris Edwards, Stonington, 1973*

*(Photo: Peter Cleary/Hedgehog House, New Zealand)*

'"Nuk" and "Pujok" at eight weeks old. The workshop was home to the pups until they were old enough to venture outdoors. Nuk and Pujok grew up together and ran as a pair throughout their working lives, forming the backbone of the Huns team.'

*Simon Gill, Rothera, and Halley 1986/92*

'Playing on the sea ice after a heavy snowfall at Rothera. The mountains of the Antarctic Peninsula and Pourquoi Pas Island can be seen in the background.'
*Simon Fraser, Rothera, 1981/84*

'At six to eight weeks the pups get their first taste of freedom and an introduction to the open white wilderness. Already the quest for strength and dominance has set in. They would seldom stray from the base huts and always roamed and hunted around in little packs. As the pups are weaned onto fatty meats., the grease sticks to their paws making them matted and dirty.'
*Simon Gill, Rothera and Halley, 1986/92*

Feeding time.                    *(Photo: Dave Burkitt, Stonington, 1974)*

'"Sonny" at about six months old. The snow outside was up to kitchen window level making it easy for an inquisitive and hungry pup to come begging for food.'
                              *Roger Owen, Adelaide, 1964*

*(Photo: Simon Fraser, Rothera, 1981/84)*

'The pups protested hugely when, at about six months of age, they were first chained to the span with the adult dogs. For twenty-four hours high-pitched howls protested against their loss of freedom. This howling suddenly stopped. On investigation the pups were found to be still howling, but no sound was coming out. They had completely lost their voices.'

*Gordon McCallum, Adelaide, 1962/63*

# CHAPTER TWELVE
# 'KURAHOUND'

*'Huskies are amazingly tough animals. My bitch "Joanna" once slipped and fell over on some hard frozen snow: I was unable to steer the loaded sledge away in time and one runner of the sledge went right over her stomach, but she got up and continued as if nothing had happened.'*

Angus Erskine, Detaille, 1956/58

Frozen and isolated, the Antarctic harbours little opportunity for disease to thrive, and with plenty of exercise, a consistent, balanced diet, and careful drivers, huskies suffered little in the way of illness and injury. The most common medical problems by far were arthritis in the older dogs, and fight injuries in the younger ones. Every effort was made to minimise both.

The law of supply and demand for the British Antarctic Survey meant that sometimes there was a doctor at base, and sometimes there wasn't. Before leaving for Antarctica, 'Fids' were therefore given extensive First Aid instruction, some written notes entitled *Kurahound,* and advised to become dab-hands with a needle and thread! For the rest, they relied on common sense. The good health of the huskies was imperative to the safety and success of field operations.

'For once "Yuri" of the Picts team had come off worst in a fight. He had a badly torn mouth and when Dr Mike Holmes operated on the living room table, we all took the opportunity to study his technique. After all, in the field, we would have to do the same on our own.'

*Rob Collister, Stonington, 1971/73*

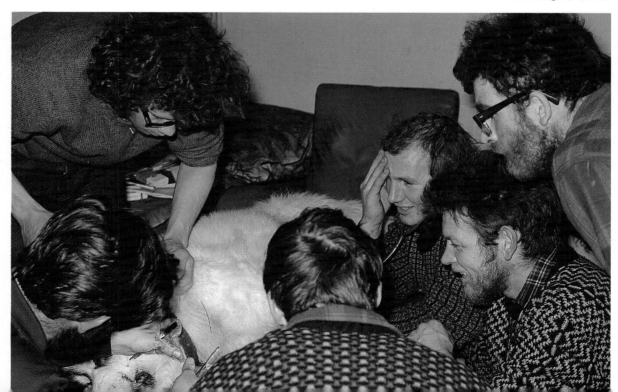

'A heavy dog could lose a quarter of his body weight when travelling, so we had to carry out regular checks. As well as this, we took blood samples for later analysis. The dogs were exceptionally tolerant of our amateurish efforts and sat patiently whilst we hunted around with a needle for the hidden veins in their forelegs. One exasperated driver was heard to say that he did not understand how his dog was alive because after numerous attempts he still could not find any blood in him.'

*Roger Scott, Stonington, 1972/75*

*(Photo: Roger Owen, Adelaide, 1963/64)*

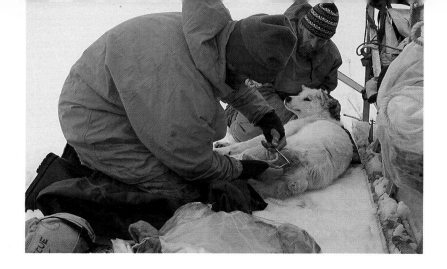

'A pleasure trip for base members finished up as a pleasure ride for sledge dog "Nuk", too. During the night Nuk had managed to slip her collar and in fighting with "Morgan" suffered a puncture wound in the left rear leg. Running the next day, the wound caused no problems until late afternoon when it started to bleed profusely. The doctor stitched her up and Nuk sat happily through the whole procedure. Dogs rarely make contented passengers so we lightly bound her rear legs with elastoplast, put her in a "stuff sack", which normally held my sleeping bag, and drew the cord up tight around her neck. Since we only had a light load Martin also rode the sledge, holding the now incapacitated but seemingly contented Nuk, to stop her slipping off the sledge. The wound healed fine, and Nuk enjoyed a couple of days being pampered in the puppy pens.'                                         *Brian Hull, Rothera, 1990/92*

It was important to inspect the dogs' feet regularly, as long claws or sharp ice crystals worked their way into the pads and could make running very painful. Some drivers made canvas booties for the dogs, which of course the dogs tried to rip off. With a seven-dog team it became an hilarious race against the clock: which one would get his booties off before the rest of the dogs were booted up? But when they started running they realised it was for their own good.

*(Photo: John Noble, Stonington, 1966/67)*

'"Briggs" was a large, red/blond-coated dog, whose name was taken from the small engine manufacturers Briggs and Stratton. It was common practice to take the dogs' names from familiar objects around base and quite often the name would be split in two to keep them short and crisp so that the dog would learn to distinguish his name from those of the rest of the team. The other advantage was that short names are easier to say when your mouth is partially frozen.

Over a period of a month or so Briggs had become really subdued. He had lost his appetite and consequently lost weight. When I went over to visit him on the spans he was depressingly listless. It came to my notice that he had developed a badly infected saliva gland in his tongue. The pain must have been excruciating, sufficient to crush even Briggs's normally impossible-to-extinguish joy of life. Something had to be done. Although understandably reluctant, the base doctor agreed to operate and remove the offending area, which was most of the right half of the floppy section of his tongue. We converted part of the sledge workshop into a temporary operating theatre and Briggs was given a general anaesthetic. Although I am not normally squeamish at the sight of blood, I felt distinctly nauseous at the sight of the doctor cutting off the offending area.

A short while after the last stitch had been tied Briggs regained consciousness. He soon staggered to his feet, stumbled determinedly across the room to a bowl of water and attempted to drink. Most of the water spilled out of the poor chap's mouth but the remaining half of the tongue was working and it didn't seem to bother him at all. A week later Briggs voluntarily held his mouth open without a murmur, while I removed the stitches from his tongue. From that moment on he never looked back. He regained all his enthusiasm for life and worked in harness for two more sledging seasons.'

*Rick Atkinson, Adelaide and Rothera, 1975/78*

'Three of us and three teams had been out of base for several days on bad sea ice. It was shortly after the lads from Horseshoe Island had gone missing, and we were all a bit nervous. Well, it happened. Ken Doyle and his team broke through into the water. We managed to drag him and the dogs out but it took us two hours, running all the way, before we reached firmer ice and were able to stop. By that time Ken's legs and feet had really frozen up and he was in a bad way. The tent erected, we thawed him out and he immediately lost the skin off both legs and feet. In our haste we had just picketed the dogs, and all of a sudden we heard a big fight erupting outside. A couple of us rushed outside and found the 30 dogs had pulled the pickets and were all scrummaging down. Once we got them sorted out, we found "Ruthie's", stomach so torn that her insides were hanging out. I pushed everything back in, roughly stitched her up and got ready to head home.

That was a hell of a journey, still on poor sea ice and with three days back to base. I led out front, with two dog teams (18 dogs), two sledges, two men – Ken could just about walk – and then Ruthie following the sorry caravan procession behind me. That night when we pitched camp, there was no sign of Ruthie. Ken was in agony and none of us could sleep. Suddenly the dogs began barking, I jumped out of my sleeping bag to investigate. It was Ruthie, dragging herself into camp. I thought I ought to put her out of her misery. But no, she'd made it this far, blood loss and all. We got back to base two days later and it took Ruthie almost another full day – but she made it. In time her belly healed and she was back to work as if nothing had happened.'

*George McLeod, Stonington, Adelaide and Fossil Bluff, 1965/68*

'"Simon", one of "Sister's" and "Bouncer's" pups, was badly bitten by a jealous bitch when he was six weeks old. Don Maclean, the American surgeon, operated to put him together. After three weeks in plaster he fully recovered and became a splendid working dog. Sadly he could not be used for breeding because, unknown to us then, he had lost his vital parts.'

*Kevin Walton, Stonington, 1945/48*

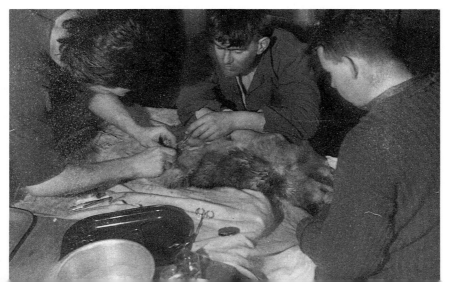

'During the winter of 1968 I was stationed at Faraday Base on the Argentine Islands where a series of dramatic and ultimately tragic events drove home the sheer isolation and vulnerability of our situation. Ken Portwine had fallen sick and through radio reports to Mike Holmes the doctor over at Stonington, ulcerative colitis was eventually diagnosed. This was bad, not least because the sea was frozen, there were no ships in the area, and no long-range aircraft could land in the limited space of the Island. For the moment there was nothing else for it but to rally round so that Ken could receive constant, if rather amateur, nursing. We all sought solace from our dogs out on the spans, where a welcome was always forthcoming, and feeding them was regarded as a reward more than a chore.

A few days later, a de Havilland Beaver made a daring and unprecedented landing on nearby Skua Island; and Argentine Dr Iturrietta and five other men were safely delivered to us. However, bad weather quickly swept in and prevented a take-off with Ken, so the situation was still critical.

About this time a dog named "Mie" was due to pup. Nothing was happening and "Doggy Man" Ian "Wink" Tyson, to whom I was assistant, became increasingly concerned. Eventually we managed to contact a Yeovil vet via Base Radio, using Radio Ham bands and a phone link, all of which was technically illegal, but we were desperate. The vet's advice amounted to giving Mie a large dose of antibiotics and a swift kick up the backside, and hope that that would produce the overdue pups. No such luck.

Eleven days later – by which time all the appropriate people had given blood transfusions to Ken – we suffered another setback. The weather cleared sufficiently for the Beaver to take off. It promptly crashed against an iceberg, and though no one was hurt, the plane was out of action indefinitely.

With everyone back on base, we began to find out the real meaning of stress and tension. Ken was now dangerously ill and we were fast running out of things we could do to help him. Mie, too, was approaching three weeks overdue and clearly in serious pain. We had already lost two dogs – "Honey", who had failed to digest a Dominican gull, and "Teviot" from old age – and the survival of Mie took on enormous significance for everyone. We all thought that here was one situation that was within our control. Dr Iturrietta, however, needed convincing, as there were ethical as well as language problems – I think he half believed we cared more for our dogs than our men! Eventually the problems were swept aside, and Iturrietta performed the operation with the assistance of seven men: three of us at the table, one man acting as translator for Iturrietta, one man receiving advice from Doc Holmes over the radio, another acting as go-between. Everyone else crossed their fingers, including Wink who proceeded to wear out the corridor pacing up and down like an expectant father.

Initially to be a caesarean, the operation turned out to be a removal of dead foetuses, but, thankfully, Mie made an extraordinarily quick recovery. Everyone's spirits rose and I suppose we came as close to celebrating as we dared under the circumstances. But the story has no happy-ever-after ending: Ken was eventually moved to hospital in Buenos Aires where he underwent two major operations. Tragically, he died shortly afterwards of peritonitis.'

*Bob Davidson, Argentine Islands, 1968/69*

Sometimes in hot weather thick-coated dogs suffered from heat stroke. The quickest cure was to make snow parcels and shove them up the dog's back end!

*(Photo: Bob Bostelmann, Stonington, 1972/74)*

'"Mitya", a rumbustious dog but one of great character, had sustained a cut on his leg in a contretemps with "Jock". A quick inspection revealed two or three stitches would form a sufficient repair job so I brought him into the shelter of the tent where I thought he would be more manageable. After a lively first few moments I managed to pin him down and insert the stitches in his leg. They were in a very awkward place and I thought I had done a really good job – until Mitya stood up and took the remains of my lilo with him. I had stitched him into it! Another frantic few minutes were spent undoing the original stitches and making good. Mitya, none the worse for my incompetence, thought it was all great fun and looked forward to the next time he was invited into the tent!'                    *Dave Fletcher, Halley, 1978*

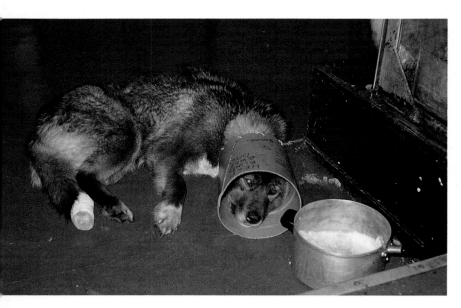

'Nig' sporting her post-operative bucket.

*(Photo: Dave Singleton, Stonington, 1972/74)*

Dogs being X-rayed for arthritis.

Veterinary surgeons Mike Godsal (1963/64) and Andy Bellars (1967/68) collaborated to work on the arthritis problem in dogs' hips and shoulders. This picture shows Bellars (right) and George McLeod taking an X-ray of pup "Gareth" with a Watson MX-' machine. Research showed that the arthritis was due to work and not to hereditary factors . Thereafter pups were not allowed to work until they were a year old.

Analysis of film taken of dogs working suggested that those with narrower hips were less likely to suffer from early osteo-arthritis. On his return to England, therefore, Bellars was promptly packed off to East Greenland, with wife in tow, to purchase six narrow-hipped dogs to improve the strain. Rumour has it the trip was their honeymoon!

*(Photo: Andrew Bellars)*

The late Eric Wilkinson, dog man at Adelaide, 1966/68, was saddled with three cases of dogs' spontaneous and uncontrollable bleeding. Fortunately this coincided with a visit by vet Andy Bellars who had to become an expert haematologist overnight. Permission was given to bring one of the affected dogs, 'Malig', to the UK to type and quantify the clotting failure. Malig was quarantined briefly in the Falklands en route for kennels near Newmarket where he was found to be suffering from haemophilia A. After careful management Malig's bleeding tendencies were controlled, and no other cases were reported in Antarctica.

*(Photo: Andrew Bellars)*

'Now we huskies do like a scrap, but it has to be said that some of the pack just don't know when to stop or when their opponent is downright beaten. For some of us, incarceration in the penitentiary is the only thing.'

*John Noble, Stonington, 1966/67*

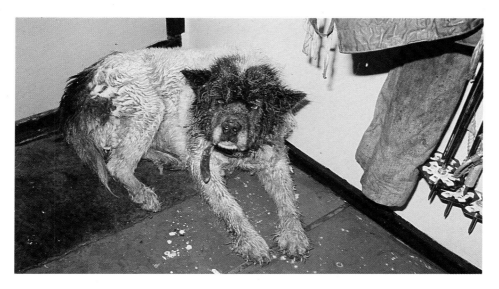

'Nedy' after a rough night.

*(Photo: Ian Sykes, Stonington, 1967/69)*

'One morning I crawled out of the tent to find that "Fury" was lying in a pool of blood on the snow. Slipping on my boots, ignoring my outer clothing, I fought my way out of the sleeve doors, and ran over to the silent tableaux. I had seen huskies recover from the most dreadful wounds, but this one was bad. I moved to lift Fury's head, taking it gently in my hands and stroking his ears. He tried to lick me but gave up after his first effort and lay still. Frank Preston helped me pick him up and we carried him into the tent. No large wounds were immediately visible, the only remarkable features being two blood icicles, about three inches long, hanging just above and behind the point of his chest bone. I hesitated to break the clotting and decided to let the icicles thaw naturally. I covered Fury with an old anorak and set about preparing the breakfast porridge. Painfully, about half a spoonful at a time, I eased some milk down his throat but he choked frequently and after a bit I gave up. Frank went outside to dig out the sledge and tent in preparation for the time when we could travel. The temperature was rising but Frank said he thought we were in for more snow and would not be able to travel for some time.

I laid in my bag trying to read a few chapters of Maigret. Even he failed to hold me. I was worried about Fury's breathing: his flanks rose and fell like bellows in short sharp gasps and he seemed desperately short of air – I presumed he was suffering "oxygen lack" from the loss of blood. As the hoar frost melted inside the tent, I used a towel to dry the groundsheet and Fury's fur as best I could – at least there was no further blood flowing. Later still, I prepared a meal and again tried spoonfeeding him, but Fury just wasn't interested. I could barely recognise the dog of yesterday and the pup of a few months before.

Fury had stood out among his brothers initially for his size, later for pure spirit. His curiosity had led him continuously into trouble. He never learnt that it was unwise to lick metal in very cold weather and on several occasions piercing screams had brought me running out to find him with his tongue stuck hard to a piece of iron. Fury it was who had egged his five brothers out to the far edge of the sea ice when it was breaking up in the early spring; they had had to be rescued from an ice-floe, each of them sitting quietly curious about his predicament. Furry had learnt the facts of life early when, at five months old, a mature dog had thrashed him for paying attention to a bitch he considered his own. Wounded, both physically and in his pride, Fury had sloped off and maintained a low profile while he recovered his courage.

I must have dozed off. Shaking my head and fixing my surroundings I realised that it was Fury's breathing that had woken me. I pumped the lamp and Frank sat up, rubbing his eyes. We looked down to see that Fury was fighting for breath. Rolling him over I saw the cause of the problem: a small hole exposing his lung which puckered and puffed as the dog fought for breath. Somehow the hole had not shown up earlier, probably blocked by frozen or clotted blood. We knelt, horribly fascinated, by the sight of this invasion of air into Fury's chest. Then I shook myself: I had to do something. I reached for the medical kit and rolled a plug of gauze. I had no experience of this and thought only to stitch the hole. It was almost impossible to stop some fur slipping past the plug into the chest cavity – the suction was acting like a vacuum cleaner. Eventually I had finished all I was capable of doing. There was no dramatic recovery. We hardly expected any now. The dog's condition seemed to deteriorate as we watched. Like a typical husky, he still fought with all his power, appearing to use every muscle in his body to breathe. But at five past four in the morning he died.

For a long time I sat on my air-bed, half relieved, totally sick with my own incompetence. Eventually I opened the tent door to look out: it was calm but snow was falling heavily, almost obscuring the light from my torch. I dressed and eased Fury's body out through the door, crawling after him. The snow shovel was standing near the door. I dug a shallow trench and laid him in it. The falling snow quickly made a shroud that covered him quietly, completely. Later that day we travelled. One space in the team a constant reminder.'

*Gordon McCallum, Adelaide, 1962/63*

Gordon McCallum enjoying happier moments with his dogs.

*(Photo: Alan Wright, Adelaide, 1961/63)*

# CHAPTER THIRTEEN
# DOG TEAMS

*'I may be guilty of painting the Moomins in "glowing" colours but they have been a splendid bunch during my term with them and have given me memories I don't think will be beaten. When you take them over, you will have a team as fine as any. Treat them how you think is best and right and most certainly you will be repaid.'*

Extract from Ben Hodges' notes to his successor, Stonington, 1964

Over the 50 years of the British Antarctic Survey, some 45 dog teams were formed and disbanded. Like football teams, each could last a long time after the lives of its individual members, with old-hands teaching youngsters the ropes until age or illness meant that they too had to be retired. Occasionally a team member would be switched, if for instance the need arose to introduce new blood; but generally the principle was, once a team member always a team member, and though individuals fought among themselves, teams would unite in force if any outsider dared to declare war. Each team had its own name, its own character and its own stories to tell. As this book shows, some of these teams became legendary.

Some teams clocked up literally hundreds of miles in a season, most notably the Terrors who started life at Hope Bay, were taken down by ship to Stonington by Noel Downham and then proceeded to travel overland from Stonington to Hope Bay and back again – a total of over 1,600 miles.

The longest recorded life span of any team seems to have been the Admirals who started life at Stonington Island base in 1958; it was dogs from this team six generations later who went to Canada in 1994. In their long life, a total of 39 dogs and 16 drivers passed through the ranks.

Six men with their team leaders on the Larsen Ice Shelf, 1964. Back left to right: Mike Fleet, geologist; Tony Marsh, geologist; Peter Kennett, geophysicist. Front left to right: Ian McMorrin with the Spartans leader 'Epsilon'; Ben Hodges with the Moomins leader 'Dot' and Ron Tindal with the Giants leader 'Lusk'.

*(Photo: Ian McMorrin, Stonington, 1962/64)*

THE MOOMINS TEAM

It is perhaps unfair to single out any team above another, but few 'Fids' will dispute the fact that the mighty Moomins saw their fair share of adventure. The team was first formed at Horseshoe Island in June/July 1958 – made up from the Greenlanders and Labradors who had gone missing out on sea ice in May of that year. Tragically their leaders Dave Statham, Stan Black and Geoff Stride were never found, but of the ten dogs who returned, 'Bessie', 'Cocky', 'Eccles', 'Alma', 'Argus', 'Coco' and 'Yana' were brought together to make up the Moomins, named after the famous Tove Jameson children's stories.

Under Ben Hodges the team was comprised as follows:

**Just some of the dog teams that have worked their way into BAS history . . .**

Admirals
Amazons
Beatles
Black Devils
Brigantes
Choristers
Chromosomes
Churchmen
Counties
Debs
Drinks
Follies
Gales
Gangsters
Giants
Guards
Gypsies
Hairybreeks
Heroes
Hobbits
Moomins
Number Ones
Old Boys
Orange Bastards
Picts
Players
Pups
Rabble
Scrags
Spartans
Terrors
Trogs
Vikings
Wogs

'DOT II'
'Very fine and sensitive leader. Easily upset when shouted at but works just as well in this reproachful condition, showing her disappointment by running with her tail down.'

'MCGRAW'
'Youngest and daftest dog in the team . . . a grand worker and very rarely slacks but sometimes takes an annoyingly long time over what should take a minute.'

'GINO'
'Extremely full of life, mischievous, inquisitive and forever bouncing around . . . Appears to thoroughly enjoy leadership. Has taken over the lead from Dot many times for short periods, either to give her a rest from heavy trail-breaking or just to keep his "paw in".'

'ARAMIS'
'Runs at second pair and fits here well . . . Does not cause any trouble but helps to keep it going.'

The team was then brought to Stonington and taken in hand by Doc Henry Wyatt, their first driver. Together with the Spartans and the Picts, the Moomins later took part in a 1,200 mile journey when the expedition's support aircraft crashed and the mechanical sledges had to be abandoned. They had to return on very low rations, nearly losing a complete team in the process. It was the Moomins who were rescued by Ben Hodges from a crevasse on Sodabread Slope, but died a year later, along with their drivers who were caught out in hurricane winds on the North-East Glacier.

'HARVEY'
'The finest dog in the team and brother to Dot . . . pulls every ounce of his 100 lb. Third pair with Eccles and they get on well together but do scrap on occasions. Will run either side but usually the left . . . Invariably the dog who sets the team "singing" with a few well timed, gentle barks.'

'ECCLES'
'An original Moomin and now the oldest member . . . He very quickly gets overweight and out of condition on base . . . eats all he can. Runs well with Harvey in third pair and should be no further forward than this position.'

'COCO'
'Definitely an individual. Cares nothing for any other dog but gets very firmly attached to any bitch he runs with.'

'FIFI'
'Back pair with Coco and enjoys his company although at times he is very clumsy in his attentions . . . If the team are howling then Fifi can be distinguished by her very strong and unladylike rendering.'

# CHAPTER FOURTEEN
# FLYING DOGS

*'The dogs seemed to enjoy aircraft travel. Sometimes they insisted on looking out of the window and occasionally a dog might fancy a shot in the pilot's seat; but we tended to discourage this practice!'*

Rick Atkinson, Adelaide and Rothera, 1975/78

Aircraft were capable of flying in polar regions as early as the 1930s, although at that time they were rarely used to carry dogs. The British Graham Land Exhibition used a Gypsy Moth biplane to survey possible sledging routes and to lay stock piles of man food, dog food and other equipment in advance of the sledging parties; and the British Antarctic Survey has always used planes of one sort or another, most notably the Auster Autocrat (Ice Cold Katy), which was lost in 1947; the Norseman Mk 5, the de Havilland Beaver, the Canso Amphibian, the de Havilland Single Otter, the Pilatus Porter, and from 1968 onwards the de Havilland Twin Otter. All these planes have proved to be well suited to polar aviation but only when in the hands of an exceptionally competent pilot. Fortunately, though BAS lost three aircraft over the years there was no loss of life. Many a plane has come to grief in the ferocious winds and snow-covered mountains of the Antarctic Peninsula. Planes were rarely flown at all during the winter months, with field parties normally travelling overland by dog team to their work areas during early spring.

The dogs always seemed to enjoy any form of travel whether it was by ship, by aeroplane or by snow vehicles: when it came to a free ride, they were quick to see the advantages of mechanical transport. Like their wolf ancestors, huskies have a highly-tuned sense of direction; even when dropped hundreds of miles from a base, they seemed to know in which direction home lay.

*'Et Nova et Vetera*
Stonington dogs with the first BAS aircraft adapted for scientific work. Though not designed to carry much cargo, she was able to support dog teams in the field. The a/c is fitted with wing-tip echo-sounding equipment which could measure the thickness of the ice over which the aircraft was flying. The picture encapsulates the technological revolution that finally displaced the dogs.'

*Dr Charles Swithinbank,*
*Stonington 1963*

'It was very crowded in the tiny plane when Knut gave the thumbs up and drew the door closed. I stood among the dogs trying to keep them calm. The noise was deafening. Suddenly to my horror I saw that "Tessy" had found a way from the cargo bay under the back seat. She was straining on her lead and snarling savagely at "Paika". Paika launched herself at Tessy but could not reach her. The excitement threw the other dogs into a frenzy. Even the best of friends were having a go at each other. I was very glad of my thick gaiters as their fangs snarled and champed at each other around my legs. The pilot was initially unaware of all this and looked amused when he eventually witnessed the scene over his shoulder. He smiled at me and gave a thumbs up. He casually increased the engine revs and lifted the helicopter straight upwards to a height of about 50 feet where he rocked and shook the aircraft violently. The dog fight stopped immediately and the terrified creatures fell to the deck and lay motionless chin to floor.'

*Nick Cox, Rothera, 1979/81*

Inside a Hercules aircraft. Four men, 21 dogs, three sledges and two months' supplies.

*(Photo: Peter Clarkson, Halley, 1969/71)*

'When flying dogs out to work in the field, the seats would be removed and dogs loaded in on top of the camping gear and sledges. The dogs would be tied on short traces and clipped individually to the sides of the fuselage in order to prevent the inevitable punch ups. The other important point was to turn the heating up high which made them lethargic and less likely to pick a fight with their next door neighbour.'

*Roger Scott, Stonington, 1972/75*

Two British Huskies arrive at Scott Base, New Zealand as part of the 1974/75 season.

*(Photo: Nick Round-Turner, Hedgehog House, New Zealand)*

'It was unusual for the dogs to relieve themselves while in the plane, especially if they weren't fed the day before they were to be flown; but the husky, when fed on seal, is renowned for its flatulence and this combined with its normal body odours could be a little overwhelming within the confinement of a plane.'

*Rick Atkinson, Adelaide and Rothera, 1975/78*

'Hey, we guys certainly get around, eh?'
Simon Gill with 'Uzra' in the 'Twotter'.

*(Photo: Simon Gill, Rothera and Halley, 1986/92)*

At the end of the 1968 field season at Stonington, all the field parties were withdrawn to base by the aircraft Pilatus Porter. On the last flight, 200 miles from home, the aircraft crashed on take-off, leaving three men, eight dogs, two sledges and all their equipment completely isolated and very short on rations. Graham Smith takes up the story:

'After discussion on the radio we decided to head for the base at Fossil Bluff on King George VI Sound. It was 150 miles away and we knew that the terrain was difficult and largely unexplored, but we hoped that the weather would be more reliable than other alternatives. All went well for the first five days but then, with 45 miles to go, in white-out conditions, the dogs suddenly stopped and refused to move on. We could not see anything wrong; the surface was a bit icy, but that was all. Anyway, we made camp and hoped the dogs would be in a better mood when the weather cleared. It eventually did clear – to reveal that we had been heading for a large crevasse, followed by a horrible ice-fall. I honestly feel that if it had not been for the sixth sense shown by Rod Ledingham's lead dog, we would have been "up the creek" in no uncertain manner.'

*Graham Smith, Stonington, 1968*

This near disaster meant that five men spent the winter in a hut built to take only four. There were virtually no dog rations, so the dogs happily made do with man food and survived! Six months later they revisited the site of the crash. In the picture below, the Vikings are seen watching with some interest as their two-legged counterparts try to retrieve goodies from a fast disappearing aircraft.

*(Photo: Ian Sykes, Stonington, 1967/69)*

# CHAPTER FIFTEEN

# SAYING FAREWELL

*'Frequently in wartime there were occasions when I had said farewell to
my family. They were always difficult; always sad; but never final for I
always expected to be back. Somehow, saying farewell to my dogs was far
worse. They had saved my life on several occasions, and, similarly, I theirs.
I wept unashamedly as I watched them from the ship that was taking me
back to civilisation. Their tails were up and they were working their hearts
out, as they always did, dragging the sledge loaded with supplies, over the
tide crack, up the hill and out of sight.'*       Kevin Walton, Stonington, 1945/48

The British Antarctic Survey has always tended to run maximum two-year tours of duty, mainly because of the potential effects incurred through living in such an isolated area for long periods of time. Having said this, arrivals and departures depended on the prevailing weather conditions, and on one or two occasions did not happen at all. In Spring 1949, for instance, sea ice, snowfall, mist and gales prevented the *John Biscoe* from approaching Stonington any closer than 200 miles. 'At last our fate was confirmed,' wrote Sir Vivian Fuchs, 'it would be another year before we saw a new face.' Thus, five of his men became the first to experience a third consecutive Antarctic winter.

In general, when the ship or aircraft did arrive, the sudden and complete change of routine and faces could in itself be nothing short of traumatic. While fledgling 'Fids' panicked about how on earth they would come to terms with their new means of transport – invariably with little more than some handwritten notes from the departing driver – it will not be hard for any dog lover to understand the intensity of feelings that the old-hands were experiencing. It was a case of saying farewell to a team with whom they had shared almost every meaningful moment of their time in Antarctica, and would almost certainly never see again. A more harrowing situation occurred when, for logistical reasons, the men were compelled to put dogs down, resulting in a sense of betrayal that can be second to none.

The Spartans team ferrying stores away from the *John Biscoe*, Back Bay, Stonington.

*(Photo: Geoff Renner, Stonington, 1964/65)*

*(Photo: Bob Bostelmann, Stonington, 1972/74)*

Trans-shipping dogs between bases always gave problems, with the ship's side way above the ice. The dogs were hauled up in special canvas lifting jackets.

'I'm not sure if the dogs truly understood what was happening as I took my last walk down the spans but I suspect they sensed some of my sorrow. At the top of the line stood "Lomond", noble and as undemonstrative as ever. In my eyes he was the most handsome and photogenic of all the dogs. It had taken a long time and a good deal of patience to gain his confidence and now I was leaving. He was inclined to shy away from any attention. To be acknowledged by a brief wag of his tail and a gentle nuzzle of his nose into my ungloved hand was as much as I could have hoped for, even on that day. We were friends and had enjoyed many an adventure together but now I was about to turn my back on him for ever. We would have travelled further if all the dogs had worked as hard and been as loyal as Lomond.

Next to Lomond, "Sue" had been barking for attention constantly since I came over to the spans. As I moved across to her I wished she could have been more sensitive on this emotional occasion. She demanded her customary rough and tumble as she frantically ran round trying to trip me over with her chain. Eventually I managed to encourage her to sit calmly with me for a while. I never felt quite the same fondness towards Sue as I did some of the others. She was a clever, reliable, hard, no-nonsense leader but I always felt her heart wasn't in the job and consequently she never found that special place in my heart. She had caused me so much grief in the early days of my time here. She really seemed to miss her previous driver and had no apparent interest in leading for me. Some dogs were like that, while others worked just as well for anyone.

Next in line were "Malky" and "Furgy", two brothers, both

biologically and in crime; they always worked just hard enough to get by. Strong, good looking dogs, of medium build, with lovely thick, dark brown coats. They would scheme together and were usually at the root of any trouble in the team, often starting it, and fighting dirty whenever possible. They wagged their tails and enjoyed the attention I gave them but would have behaved the same had anyone come to visit.

On to "Briggs", one of my all-time favourites. An honest dog if ever there was one. Never to be a leader but always a worker. No fuss, he just got on with what had to be done. I felt he understood that I was leaving and that someone else would take my place. He would endure the consequences, just as he had done with me. It felt to me that we were communicating on a subliminal level about all the events of the past as I sat beside him. It was some time before I moved on.

"Boot" was a white, ugly kind of a dog. He was pals with Briggs and enjoyed being beside him on the spans. He always warbled rather than barked, in his peculiar way, and today was no exception. As he stood there looking at me, I thought he looked more like a British bulldog than a husky. His legs were too short and his chest was too wide. His stump of a tail was wagging, the part that remained after one of his more serious battles. I felt fond of this dog, not because he worked hard but because he was amusing. He was the dog that things seemed to happen to. He would be the one to break through thin sea ice, or the one that fell into a crevasse or the one that always came off worse in a fight. Nothing bothered him. All the funny moments I had shared with the dogs came rushing back as I said farewell to Boot.

Next in line was "Lil", my favourite and "the Rothera tart". As always when anyone was over at the spans she was jumping four feet in the air time after time. With every leap her front paws went back and forth under her three or four times, scooping in the air, in an attempt to pull the visitor towards her. On my reaching her she jumped up into my arms and would stay there for as long as she could. She was a diminutive bundle of irrepressible energy: what she lacked in size she made up for in spirit. The thought of that little dog jumping over snow drifts for mile after mile out on the trail, while the other larger dogs were able to plough through, still brings tears to my eyes. Despite her size she pulled with the force of two and was always the first to try to start the sledge after a break. I would miss Lil, more than all the rest.

Last but one along the line stood "Helix" the aristocrat. His strong, distinctive bark had been demanding attention for some time. Now at last he could stand on his hind legs with his front paws resting on my shoulders, as was his way, while we had a good long chat about my departure. Helix was the largest of the dogs in the team, but a gentle giant. He enjoyed human company more than most of the dogs and I enjoyed being with him. It was Helix that I took for walks along the beach when I wanted a confidant with whom to talk. Again, as with Briggs, I sensed that Helix could tell this was farewell.

Last in line stood the mighty "Argus", the undisputed chief. Large and muscular, dark brown in colour and lion-like in stature. He had always seemed different from the rest. He had sat impassively, almost embarrassed, while I made a fuss of all the other dogs. It was appropriate that I should say "So long" to Argus last of all. I had never felt at ease with him and sensed that he didn't hold me in very high esteem. I petted him and started to play fight as we often would, trying to disguise my true feelings. As we rolled on the ground I became aware of a warm sensation running down my neck, inside my anorak hood. Simultaneously the sensation and the smell confirmed my suspicions. Argus had peed on me – the ultimate expression of contempt!'

*Rick Atkinson, Adelaide and Rothera, 1975/78*

As bases were closed down, the difficult situation sometimes arose where new homes could not be found for the dogs, as David Dalgliesh recalls here:

'When it came to the time of my departure, many of our dogs had to be culled. Though we all felt it was the ultimate betrayal we traded on their failing for food – a fresh piece of meat lying in the snow and a .45 bullet in the head. It fell to my lot to dispatch old "Grandfather Snipe", one of the original dogs who had come down from Labrador. He bent down to eat his meat and then a strange thing happened. He dropped it, lifted his head and looked me straight in the eye as if to say, "Well, I've been reprieved so often, I can take what's necessary. I won't make it difficult for you."'

*David Dalgliesh, Stonington, 1948/50*

(Photo: Ian Sykes, Stonington, 1967/69)

[overleaf]
(Photo: Ben Osborne, Rothera, 1989/92)

# CHAPTER SIXTEEN
# HONORARY RETIREMENTS

*'By 1967, when my turn had come to leave Antarctica, "Mac" of the Terrors was becoming progressively slower with a limp that might have been arthritis, or possibly the result of undetected injury at the time of a crevasse accident. It seemed to me that he was a dog of magnificent temperament as well as physique, and I couldn't bear the thought of seeing him put down. Added to that, I discovered that his sledging mileage totalled an astonishing 14,440 miles — perhaps an all-time record. Armed with this fact, and with a liberal allowance of sentiment, I approached the authorities and after much discussion and dire warnings about "pet" huskies, I was granted permission to take Mac back with me to England and a warmer climate.'*
Dave Matthews, Signy and Stonington, 1964/66

In the first 30 years of the British Antarctic Survey, dogs were so much a part of life that there was a tendency to forget that they had to earn their keep as working dogs. Freighting huskies were at their peak at four or five years old; as they grew older so their ability to pull grew less, and eventually they were withdrawn from the team. Some were put down; some were sent as breeding sires to the smaller island bases; whilst a select few were given honorary retirement — accompanying their drivers to new worlds beyond the snow. They have their own stories to tell.

'Darkie' with Peter Fuchs, Sir Vivian Fuchs' son.

'Darkie, my lead dog, was among a team of nine who came back to England, to play a part in the Polar Pavilion during the 1953 Festival of Britain. They gave over 2,000 sledging performances for the public. They were a great draw . . . Afterwards Darkie came to live with me in Cambridge where he became a well-known figure. He always wove a careful course through the traffic as he hauled me on a bicycle, ever punctilious in obeying commands regarding the lights. But it took a long time to teach him not to jump the white lines, which *he* knew to be "crevasses" in the tarmac.'

*Extract from* Of Ice and Men
*by Sir Vivian Fuchs*

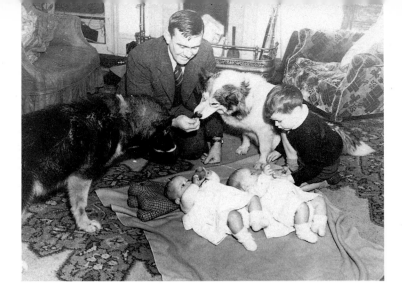

Kevin Walton, with huskies 'Darkie' and 'Sister' watching over his three children Jonathan, Myra and Jane.

'"Sister" was conceived in Antarctica in 1949 and born in England where her mother and 30 other dogs were being quarantined for onward passage to the Norwegian British Swedish Expedition to Queen Maude Land. She was one of two puppies to survive an attack of hardpad. When she was a bit older I took her to work with me at the Nuclear Power Station construction site at Trawsfynydd, North Wales, and she became our mascot there. She had a mind of her own and was never cured of killing chickens and chasing sheep; but our family of four children grew up very happily with her around.

In 1950 I was asked by the embryonic "Husky Club of Great Britain' whether I would mate Sister with a husky that had been brought into England at the end of the war by G P Jordan. We arranged things by telegram but the nature of Chinese Whispers being what it is, the message handed in at the village Post Office read "To Jordan. District Youth Welfare Officer West Yorkshire. Please postpone your visit one week as my sister is not yet ready for mating". It was received with somewhat raised eyebrows.

Sister later had pups by the famous Darkie. One of these was "Gino", who grew up to become the mascot of the Aberdovey Outward Bound Mountain Rescue team. His greatest claim to fame was that he once located a Welsh Collie on the north-west slopes of Cadair Idris, hitherto lost for six days. Sadly Gino eventually had to be put down for attacking the school gardener who mercilessly taunted him, assuming that Gino was always tethered. One day he wasn't and Gino had an unforgiving nature.'

*Kevin Walton, Stonington, 1945/48*

'Sister' at Talyllyn, North Wales.

Sister had another pup who became something of a legend in his lifetime . . .

'When Launcelot Fleming, a bachelor, onetime geologist and padre to the BGLE, became Bishop of Portsmouth, he inherited a dog – "Dusky the Husky". It happened that I, the bishop's domestic chaplain, was away at the time, and on my return found that Dusky had been sentenced to spend most of his time at the end of a chain secured to the wall of a rather small yard. The cook was up in arms because tradesmen were too terrified to make deliveries and the aptly named Budd the gardener was equally aggrieved because he was expected to clear up the abundant droppings. Dusky very obviously required more freedom than the yard allowed but, equally obviously, he could not be allowed to roam free. A wooden stake was hammered into the garden lawn and a long rope attached. That proved to be useless because Dusky's pulling power, as befits a dog bred to the sledge, was a good deal greater than was the security of the stake. Very soon Dusky reappeared in the kitchen yard, towing the rope with the stake at its end. His route was obvious: there was a trail of destruction.

A husky must nevertheless have exercise, and it fell upon me, newly ordained, to take Dusky for his walk. Tentatively, I placed Dusky on the front passenger seat of my car, drove him to a less populous area, let him out, and then drove on, leaving him to lope along behind. Dusky enjoyed this, but equally he enjoyed the drive back, taking an interest in the passing scene and occasionally

lending a heavy paw to the steering wheel or the gear lever, or trying to share my seat. It was all somewhat hazardous so Dusky was transferred to the backseat. The doors had lever handles, and Dusky, although not the most intelligent of creatures, soon discovered that a paw on these would release the door and out he could go. Fair enough in the country but most inconvenient in town. So Dusky was brought back to the front seat. A *modus vivendun* eventually was reached. In place of the saloon I bought a two-seater which had secure door fastenings. After that there was only one incident. An irate woman accused me of cruelty to animals because I was making my dog run behind the car. "That," she said, "will exhaust him." I told her that I was the one who was exhausted.

Launcelot Fleming's bedroom had a balcony which provided suitable night quarters for Dusky. There, in an outsize basket, he took his rest, reclining when the bishop went to bed and rising when he heard the bath water being run. When his owner was away bedroom doors had to be left open so that Dusky could come from his basket, through the bishop's bedroom, along the passage and into my bedroom. Sometimes a bit of a cuddle and some comforting words would satisfy him and he would return to his basket. More frequently he would decide to share my bed for the remainder of the night. Of course Dusky was much better than a hot water bottle in winter, less agreeable when the weather was warm. And summer or winter it left little of the bed for me. Dusky required a good deal of space.

Outward bound with 'Gino', North Wales.

*(Photo: Vernon Walker)*

One day Dusky disappeared. In late afternoon there was a telephone call from the local police station. A dog, a cross between an Alsatian and a Pomeranian, wearing a collar on which was the bishop's address, had been brought in. Did we claim it? Much relieved, I went to the police station and was taken through to the yard where stood an outsize and very secure kennel. "Very dangerous," warned the policeman, standing back, "you'd better be careful." I unlocked the door and out loped Dusky; he reared up on his hindlegs and licked my face. I proceeded to give the policeman a lecture on the difference between a husky and a cross between an Alsatian and a Pomeranian – if such an unlikely animal did in fact exist – put a well deserved fiver into the charity box, and took Dusky home. That, I thought, was that. It was not.

Next day, another policeman was presented at my study door. Had I failed to respect the 30 mph limit? Or perhaps something even more dreadful?

"Are you the owner of an Alsatian crossed with a Pomeranian?" the policeman asked.

I replied that I was not.

"His Lordship has just told me that you collected the dog from the police station."

"Yes, I collected a husky."

"Were you aware that the dog took and ate a chicken from the poultry farm?"

"No," I said. "I was not aware of that. May I pay compensation?"

I handed over another fiver, and the policeman smiled, closed his notebook and departed. I doubt the poultry keeper received as much as five pounds for any other of his chickens.

I left some time later for my new parish, and when I visited Bishopswood, there was no Dusky. I learned that he had been dispatched to Antarctica after he had created a snowstorm of the contents of the bishop's down duvet. The place did not feel the same for he really was a most endearing dog and a real friend. The bishop left soon afterwards, too. In his new diocese he had a Dachshund.'

*The Reverend Eric Staples*

Footnote: Dusky worked hard as a sledge-puller. He should have been used as a sire but his dog card records that 'Dusky is utterly uninterested in bitches on heat'. His celibate upbringing had caught up with him.

'In 1972, at the age of nine months, "Rasmus" was retired to Fossil Bluff, a small four-man wintering base that used mechanical vehicles as their mode of transport. Sometimes Rasmus travelled with us as a mascot, slumped across a load, near the back of the sledge. In tricky terrain, a karabiner was attached to his collar and was clipped to the sledge lashings. Once, while crossing smooth snow at 15-20 miles per hour, Rasmus fell off the sledge, but the karabiner held and Rasmus's old legs were forced to go like they'd never gone before.

Rasmus was great company. You could take him for walk – not too fast, mind – and pour out all the annoyances that accumulated at the one-room base – he was a good listener! In fact, there was only one time when we regretted having him around. The base used to receive a complimentary turkey at Christmas time and one year the much drooled over bird disappeared from the table where it had been defrosting. "What, me?" Rasmus seemed to be saying when we looked at him with incrimination in our eyes.

Rasmus died quite suddenly on 1st August 1974. He was 12 years and four months old – perhaps the oldest husky in BAS history. Fossil Bluff was a poorer place for his going.'

*Jonathan Walton, Fossil Bluff, 1973/75*

'Rasmus' with Roger Tindley at Fossil Bluff.    *(Photo: Jim Bishop, Fossil Bluff, 1972/75)*

'Mac' in the hills near Pitlochry, Scotland 1968.

"'Mac" was born at Hope Bay on 30th October 1958, and ran as a pair with his brother "Bryn" in the Terrors. Most of their sledging was done without the support of aircraft which made life so much easier for dog teams in later years. Not for them the comfortable flight to a work area and the convenient food depots nearby. It was back-breaking depot-laying trips when all that counted were load, speed and distance – the familiar price to be paid for the rare days when a lightly laden sledge glided effortlessly over crisp snow and sledging was pure pleasure.

. . . Following my battle with the "immigration" authorities and the long voyage to England, Mac and I lived for the first month or so in Birmingham. I had great fun watching his adjustment to "civilisation", and seeing things through his eyes. Up to the age of eight and a half, he had seen only rock, snow, men, penguins, seals and a few birds. Grass and vegetation were obviously extraordinary and fascinating at first; women and children really confused him; while all four-legged animals from Pekinese to horses were – to my relief – virtually ignored as "non-husky". One yapping terrier came at him with intent to do battle, but Mac picked his moment to lift his back leg and replied with a devastatingly accurate aim, almost drowning the poor animal. To the many questions concerning what I fed Mac, I developed two stock replies: either "A brace of poodles a day", or, "I just drive him into the pet shop and say 'Fill 'im up!'"

After Birmingham, my work as a survey geologist took me to the Scottish Highlands for four years and Mac lived with me there, sleeping under my caravan. He had the usual husky habit of howling at the moon and of wishing to chase other animals but was fortunately ineffective at the latter thanks to developing arthritis in his back legs. I was castigated once or twice by unknown members of the public for having a "dangerous dog"; but in fact I think it was myself who was more in danger of being attacked – by the companions of mini-skirted girls who, on the rare occasions I had Mac on a crowded pavement, felt a cold damp nose performing an ungentlemanly but very doggy act!

Our stay by a fishing hotel gave some amusing moments. I was regularly supplied with a bucket of scraps for Mac. One evening a new waitress approached my caravan with the eagerly awaited bucket. Evidently she had not been warned what to expect and when Mac came bounding up to her she dropped the bucket and fled in terror. He ate the entire bucketful in less than a minute. The waitress soon recovered her composure (and her bucket) and was duly instructed in the art of bellowing "Lie down" as if she meant it.

During my time in Scotland, I attended a snow training course and took part in several major searches with the Search and Rescue Dog Association (then in its infancy). There was certainly no problem with Mac's ability to work in severe weather and he was quite happy in conditions which turned the more widely used Alsatians and Collies into shivering wrecks. He could also detect and follow faint air scents over snow as well, if not better, than the others. The problem came with trying to teach an old dog new tricks, for Mac had no instinct whatsoever to obey commands for a systematic search or to bark at significant finds. One of the early exercises for a trainee avalanche search dog is to bury the dog's owner/handler in a shallow snow "grave" and to get the dog to find him by scent. Mac found me all right, but instead of barking and digging he simply lifted his leg for a pee and walked off! I've often wondered what precisely was going through his doggy mind at that point.

On occasion I would go rock climbing, particularly in the mountains of the Isle of Skye, and I would tether Mac to a rock at the start of the climb. He never tried to escape, but was liable to raise a tremendous racket of howling to register his protest. The sound would echo around the peaks, as it must have done in ancient times when wolves lived in Scotland.

All in all, I think Mac had a very enjoyable retirement. He died, sadly without descendants, at the age of eleven and a half, just as his general condition was beginning to decline. It happened under anaesthetic for an emergency operation on intestinal torsion, and left me feeling sad but relieved that his end was quick, painless and not undignified. I buried him on a Welsh hill.'

*Dave Matthews, Signy and Stonington, 1964/66*

'Bagging' Munros in the northern Highlands.

# CHAPTER SEVENTEEN

# PHASING OUT

*'I realise that there are good things to be achieved by Skidoos, but the soul requires that the field season is not purely work, work, work. It is nice to think that you have undemanding, loyal friends outside the tent, who will do your bidding in payment for a block of Nutty at the end of the day, and that a bit more effort can always be achieved with a shout and a whistle. Not so the skidoo.'*

Chris Edwards, Stonington, 1973/75

Mechanical vehicles, most notably the Muskeg tractor and the vintage military Weasel, have been pulling heavy loads over short distances; in Antarctica since the early 1930s; but the first machine with the potential to replace dog teams for long distances was the Eliason motor toboggan, introduced in 1961. On firm surfaces this machine could pull considerable loads at about 15 miles per hour – about twice the speed of dogs. However, in soft snow and in crevassed terrain the Eliasons proved extremely dangerous as they tended to dig their way through snow bridges with disastrous results. As well as this they frequently broke down. Such was the contempt in which they were held, 'Fids' nicknamed them 'Elsans', the trade name of a well known brand of portable chemical toilets.

In August 1963 the following fax was sent to the men at Stonington Base:

'With the increasing emphasis on the use of mechanical aids to travel by BAS the future of dogs has been reviewed by London and it has been decided that no more breeding is to take places on bases except at Halley Bay who must plan to maintain three teams indefinitely.'

'Rubbish!' replied the men. 'What emphasis?' The contempt was indicative of a loyalty to the dogs that went beyond their efficiency as sledge-pullers, for these machines posed a major threat to the romance and challenge of travel in Antarctica, and inevitably it was only a matter of time before technology overtook the dogs altogether.

In 1957 Sir Vivian Fuchs and Sir Edmund Hillary had used three modified Ferguson tractors, four four-track Tuckernan Sno-Cats, three Weasels, as well as two dog teams, on their record-breaking 2,180-mile, 99-day journey across Antarctica – Shackleton's attempt in 1914-17 had been a disaster and they were taking no chances. Driven by Ken Blaiklock and Jon Stephenson, the dogs played a major role as route finders in difficult terrain. It was not until 1989 that a six-man, six-country expedition, led by American Will Steger and Frenchman Jean Louis Ettiene, made the trans-Antarctic traverse relying solely on dogs and aircraft support, with ex-BAS man Geoff Somers as principal dog driver. They achieved the crossing in seven months and all 40 dogs survived.

By the early 1970s the 640 cc two stroke Bombardier Alpine Twin Track Skidoos had proved themselves to be safe, reliable and vastly more cost effective than dogs and the earlier Eliasons. Combined with improved aircraft support, it became possible to complete in two months the type of field work that had once taken two years. Ever-increasing commercial pressures meant that few scientists could justify devoting their valuable work time to the relative slowness of travel by dog team; and over the next 20 years dog numbers were reduced from around 200 in 1972 to a mere 30 in 1992.

In the early days at Rothera, when dogs were being phased out, there were about 50 dogs making up five teams: the Admirals, the Gaels, the Huns, the Picts and the Players. Keeping the dogs was regarded as a privilege and on the understanding that there should be no expense to BAS. The official line was that when the dog food ran out the dogs would have to go. In order to prevent this happening, the stocks of Nutrican stored at the depots along the Peninsula were removed whenever a flight was returning empty, and added to the dwindling supply at base. To bolster supplies still further, sledging rations left over from other expeditions were sent south by those concerned for the dogs' future.

On numerous occasions it was suggested that as huskies were no longer required for field work they should be removed altogether, and the debate regarding the relative virtues of Skidoo and dog was never far from conversation. But even the most ardent of mechanics had a soft spot in their hearts for the dogs and when it came to recreation there were many that preferred to travel by dog team than by noisy, smelly Skidoo. Although most of the dog travel was restricted to winter and spring, some remarkable mileages were achieved. In the years that the sea froze many a journey was made in the footsteps of the British Graham Land Expedition, exploring nooks and crannies in the fjords of Marguerite Bay, finding the country still pristine and full of wonder. It was on these journeys that friendships were bonded that will last a life time. Sir Vivian Fuchs once noted how many dog drivers became so totally obsessed with their teams that girlfriends back home frequently complained 'their messages are never about me – only about the damned dogs.'

Certainly the arguments for maintaining dogs for morale and recreational purposes were considerable. Indeed, they were to hold the day until 1994 when new protocol agreed amongst the members of the Antarctic Treaty engineered the dogs' eviction altogether.

The 'mechanical dog' – Eliason motor toboggan, introduced in 1961.

'In certain conditions Eliasons were wonderful; they could haul loads straight up the steep lower section of "Sodomy Slope". But in other conditions they developed a form of wheelspin. It was a sort of tortoise and hare act until they finally broke down and were abandoned.'

*Ben Hodges, Stonington, 1961/64*

Sledge down a crevasse.

(Photo: British Antarctic Survey Archives)

'During a local journey from Stonington Island a group of us got off route in the heavily crevassed foot of the Swithinbank Glacier. I was leading with the Ladies when my colleague called from behind that one of his dogs had dropped in a hole. I stopped and stupidly took my skis off. Only a few paces from my sledge I found myself up to the armpits in the bridge of a huge crevasse. My sledge also dropped back into it at the same time. All I could see below me was blackness. Because I hadn't picketed the dogs, I was able to call old "Shirl" over, grab her harness and pull myself out – not something I could have asked a Skidoo to do!'

*Dave Singleton, Stonington, 1972/74*

*(Photo: Jim Bishop, Fossil Bluff, 1972/75)*

Taken in October 1974, this picture marks the end of an era – the last unsupported dog journey from Stonington, travelling across the Plateau to Alexander Island.

*(Photo: Jonathan Walton, Fossil Bluff, 1973/75)*

On George VI Ice Shelf the Stonington dog teams met up with a four-person mechanised wintering party from Fossil Bluff. In this scene there are dogs, Skidoos and a Muskeg tractor. The next day 'old' and 'new' parted company, each to continue its own programme of scientific work. Skidoos were now fitted with larger engines and, as long as they worked in pairs, were deemed 'reliable' enough to replace dogs for field work.

'In days of old when "Fids" were bold
And Muskegs weren't invented,
Men used dogs instead of cogs
And lived their lives contented.'

*Peter Clarkson, Halley, 1968/75*

*(Photo: Dave Singleton, Stonington, 1972/74)*

A broken-down Skidoo – there was nothing a dog driver enjoyed more than to return to base with a broken Skidoo loaded onto his sledge.

# CHAPTER EIGHTEEN
# OF DOGS AND DIPLOMATS

*'It is sad to reflect that, in an attempt to achieve the unattainable goal of perfection in the protection of the Antarctic environment, the dogs should have become legislative pawns in the game of "green" politics.'*

Peter Clarkson, Halley, 1968/75

Antarctica is a fragile continent. Each year the protective ozone layer becomes a little thinner, the globe a little warmer and, in consequence, the ocean a little larger. The threat to the environment is considerable, and certainly measures must be taken to protect it.

In 1991, under pressure from environmentalists, a new clause was incorporated into the Antarctic Treaty.

'INTRODUCTION OF
NON-NATIVE SPECIES,
PARASITES AND DISEASES

Dogs shall not be introduced onto land or
ice shelves and dogs currently in those areas
shall be removed by April 1, 1994.'

The rationale behind this legislation was to protect the Antarctic seal populations from infection by a distemper-like virus, such as that which affected the North Sea seal population around the British coasts. It would appear however that a distemper-like virus is already endemic in seals. In 1955 7,000 of them died from it on the sea ice near Hope Bay. Naturally dogs were an obvious target for blame but subsequent tests proved conclusively that they were clean. Seals are wide-ranging animals and many of them visit other southern continents; it seems plausible that the virus could have been contracted directly or indirectly from infected animals there. In any case, vaccination against distemper is now a routine procedure for all puppies.

So why did the Antarctic Treaty insist on the removal of dogs? Huskies, like all animals, must be fed, and the most convenient and satisfactory food supply has traditionally come from the local seal population. Even so, when you consider the crabeater seal population is already of the order of 12,000,000 and is growing not decreasing, it seems unlikely that there has been any real impact on seal numbers from this practice. Perhaps the concern was focused more on the fact that dogs have to relieve themselves like any other animal and in doing so might discolour the snow. It would be difficult to measure the level of pollution created by even a thousand huskies when spread over the five million square miles of the Antarctic – men and mechanical vehicles have already proved to be far more effective polluters. Probably the real answer to the question is that it was a pointless piece of legislation which slipped through under a smokescreen of more important issues.

Few, if any of the bureaucrats instrumental in the eviction of the huskies from Antarctica had any appreciation of the value of the relationship that existed between man and dog in this lonely continent. One thing is for sure: there will be no more dog tracks in the snows of Antarctica for some time to come.

Joining the 'Touch the whale' club.
During the 1955 seal epidemic, Killer Whales took to using the seals' breathing holes. Some of them would even allow themselves to be petted, but for dogs these were strictly 'no go' areas.

*(Photo: A F Lewis, Hope Bay, 1955)*

A lamp post 'borrowed' from a London Park and well patronised by the dogs at Rothera.

*(Photo: Nick Cox, Rothera, 1979/81)*

# CHAPTER NINETEEN

# THE LAST GENERATION

*'The Inuit were delighted to see the dogs running on the traditional fan trace and to hear the commands still spoken in their language. They hoped that our dogs would allow them to recapture a part of their cultural heritage.'*

John Sweeny, Rothera, 1993/94

By 1993 only two teams remained in Antarctica, the Admirals and the Huns, and one final, momentous journey awaited them – Operation 'Home For the Huskies', which would take them thousands of miles back to their origins on the other side of the world. By way of a 'thank you' the dogs were given one last season out in the field – a trip led by John Sweeny, the last dog man at Rothera, and John Killingbeck, who had worked with the dogs 30 years earlier at Adelaide Island. Their objective was to measure the climatic differences between the east and west side of Alexander Island – a poignant reminder that it is the issue of global warming that now must dominate our pursuit of Antarctica's secrets. Back at Rothera, everyone made the most of the dogs' company before giving them an emotion-filled send-off in the BAS Dash 7 aircraft on 22nd February, 1994.

Organised by John Hall, Operations Manager of BAS, and sponsored by bodies too numerous to mention, it was John Sweeny who, quite literally, became the driving force behind the project to find new homes for the huskies. Following quarantine in Port Stanley on the Falkland Islands, Sweeny accompanied the dogs to Heathrow Airport, then on to Boston, where a truck drove them to Hudson Bay in Canada. From here, Sweeny joined forces with Americans Polly Mahoney and Kevin Slater and together they drove the dogs overland to new homes in Inukjuak, a distance of 300 miles, where they were met with a huge and enthusiastic welcome.

It was hoped that the 'last generation' would in fact be the 'new generation', not just for the dogs of the British Antarctic Survey, but for the Inuit Eskimos, too. In the 1950s and 60s the Royal Canadian Mounted Police had adopted an unexplained policy of exterminating dogs they found roaming loose, and the valuable strain upon which the Eskimos depended for survival, was in danger of being lost altogether. Tragically, this was not to be. Outside the sterile environment of Antarctica, some of the dogs succumbed to various infections, and attempts to breed those that survive appear to be failing. The line of dogs to which Britain owes so much of her pioneering polar heritage, looks set to die out.

'"Pujok" was six and a half years old, and during our final journey was diagnosed as having osteo-arthritis. We gave her painkiller in her food, and let her sleep on the safety pup tent on the sledge. Sadly she never really recovered. She made the journey, but had to be put down when we reached the Falklands. Another dog, "Rex", was thought to be too old to make the journey and he was left behind at Rothera. He wasn't at all happy about this. He howled and howled for his companions until one of the pilots stationed there took pity on him. Rex was returned to the team and eventually made it to Canada.'

*John Killingbeck, Rothera, 1993/94*

The old and the new. The new BAS Dash 7 aircraft, piloted by Peter Buckley, flies over the Huns and the Admirals on the Wright Peninsula. Two days later the aircraft was used to fly the dogs to the Falkland Islands on their journey to new homes in North America.

*(Photo: Charlie Siderfin, Rothera, 1992/94)*

*(Photo: John Killingbeck, Rothera 1993/94)*

The final journey for dogs in Antarctica.
Passing Ellsworth Mountains, November 1993.

Dr Charlie Siderfin coaxes 'Roy' aboard the Dash 7. Operation 'Home for the Huskies' captured the public's attention, and film crew attended all the stop-off points on the journey.

*(Photo: John Sweeny)*

'A very large proportion of the village of Inukjuak had turned out to greet us, and much handshaking and introductions took place. Many of the older folk were quite emotionally affected and there were a few wet eyes.'

John Sweeny, Rothera, 1993/94

*(Photo: Louis Molgat)*

*[overleaf]*
Evensong at Adelaide.
*(Photo: Geoff Renner, Stonington, 1964)*

181

# DOG NUMBERS

DOGS APPEARING ON BAS RECORDS
BETWEEN 1945 AND 1994                                          c. 900


IMPORTED
Labrador, 1946                                                      75

British North Greenland Expedition, 1954                           20

England, born of Antarctic Husky stock, 1954                        3

East Greenland, 1969                                                6

Exchanged with stock from New Zealand
and Argentinean field stations, late 1970s                          4

Total                                                             108

BORN IN ANTARCTICA                                             c. 850


DEATHS ON FIELD JOURNEYS
Crevasse accidents                                                 40

Drowned                                                            25

Fight wounds / lost on trail / natural causes                      30


EXPORTED
Festival of Britain / Queen Maude Land Expedition                  45

'Retired' as domestic pets to Britain and
South Africa                                                        3

Exchanged with stock from New Zealand
and Argentinean field stations, late 1970s                          4

Sent to North Canada, 1994                                         14

# A FAMILY TREE OF BAS DOGS

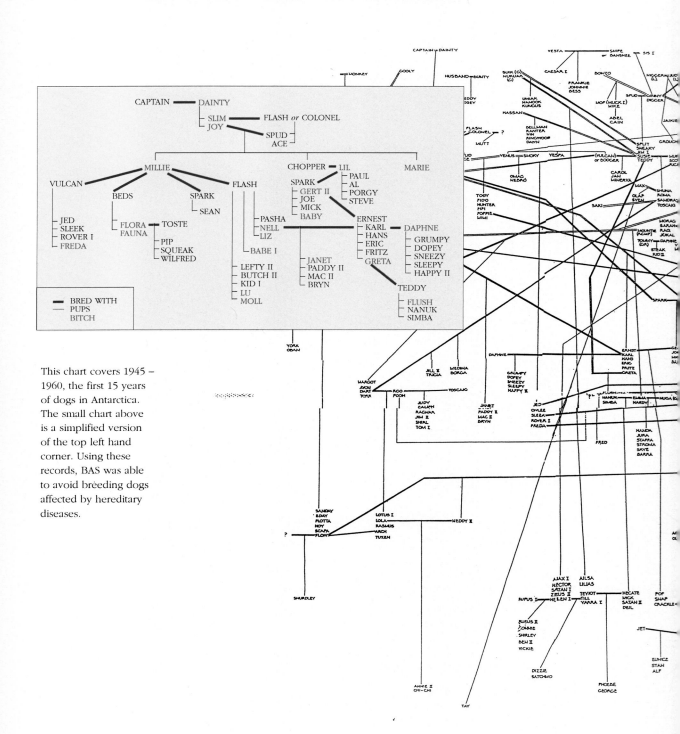

This chart covers 1945 –
1960, the first 15 years
of dogs in Antarctica.
The small chart above
is a simplified version
of the top left hand
corner. Using these
records, BAS was able
to avoid breeding dogs
affected by hereditary
diseases.

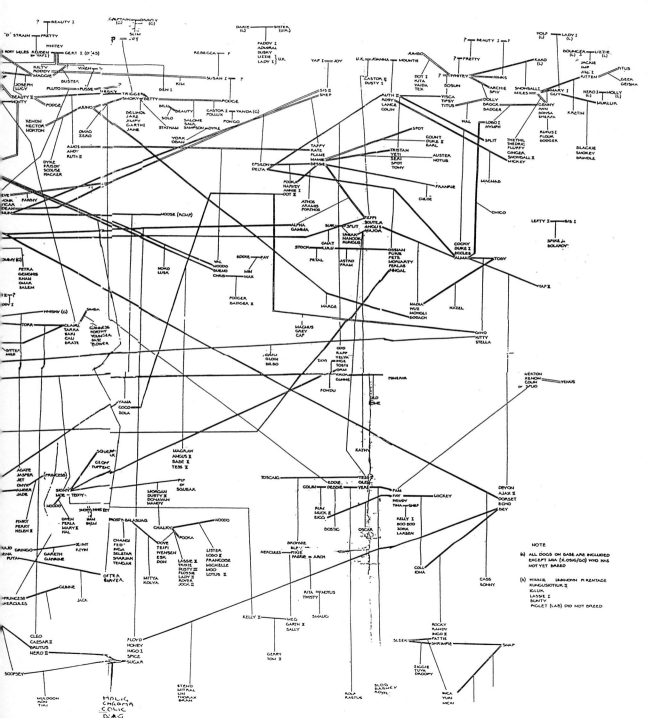

NOTE

(a) ALL DOGS ON BASE ARE INCLUDED EXCEPT MIA (X.OSIG/GO) WHO HAS NOT YET BRED

(b) WINNIE    UNKNOWN PARENTAGE
    KUNGUSIOTIUK II
    KILLUM
    LASSIE I
    BUNTY
    PIGLET (LAB) DID NOT BREED

185

# MILEAGES

APPROXIMATE TOTAL MILEAGES BY DOG TEAMS      336,500

| | |
|---|---:|
| Hope Bay and View Point (15 years) | 69,000 |
| Stonington (20 years) | 180,000 |
| Detaille (3 years) | 4,000 |
| Adelaide (16 years) | 16,000 |
| Halley (19 years) | 35,000 |
| Horseshoe Island (5 years) | 4,300 |
| Rothera (16 years) | 15,000 |
| Argentine Islands, Admiralty Bay, Deception Island, Prospect Point, Signy, Anvers I and Fossil Bluff | 6,000 |

| | |
|---|---:|
| Longest unsupported 'one way' journey, 1947 | 700 in 67 days |
| Slowest unsupported 'one way' journey, 1957 | 200 in 53 days |
| Average distance covered by individual dogs | 3,000 |
| Longest distance covered by individual dogs ('Mac' and 'Bryn', both born at Hope Bay in 1958) | 14,440 |

# INDEX